MW01039775

Meal Prep Magic

Meal Prep Magic

✳ Time-Saving Tricks for
Stress-Free Cooking

Catherine McCord

Photography by Colin Price

ABRAMS, NEW YORK

Contents

Preface

"Every time I open my fridge is a reminder of how f*%#ed up my life is."
—a good friend, who shall remain anonymous

Raison d'Être

My friend proclaimed this statement above to me one day not too long ago, and her words totally floored me. She's so right, I thought. Money, status, possessions, work/life balance—they're all inadequate metrics for determining how we feel about our lives. Rather, what you see each time you open the door to your fridge (or freezer or pantry) can be a surprisingly accurate, tangible barometer of self-worth, or at least I'm finding that it is in the mom circles in which I travel. It dawned on me that, for so many of us, the difference between an organized kitchen (i.e., everything you need always exactly where it should be, meals prepped and sorted for the week, zero clutter) and a disorganized one (i.e., none of the aforementioned attributes) can mean the difference between having a healthy and empowered sense of self, versus being consumed by stress and self-loathing. After spending the majority of twenty-four months confined to my home, surrounded constantly by family, and trying to figure out what our new normal was going to be like, the idea for this book came to me.

The Magical Connection Between Organization, Meal Prep, and Inner Peace

Comparing the state of your life and your fridge is an obvious (and intentionally humorous) simplification; however, there is also undoubtedly a kernel of truth to the analogy. When I open my refrigerator or pantry, I'm not kidding when I say that what I encounter (well stocked, neatly organized, and prepped so that I can find whatever I need when I'm rushing to make breakfast, school lunches, or dinner, OR the contents arranged pell-mell, requiring me to rummage for an ingredient I need and either not find it or realize someone in my family never mentioned that they finished it) can dictate whether I feel calm and confident, or frazzled and frustrated, and I think I can speak for most of us when I say this feeling has a major impact on our ability to accomplish what needs to be done.

I know I'm not alone when I say that one of my biggest overall stresses is realizing that it's five P.M. and that I've got no (expletive deleted) idea what I'm doing for dinner. It doesn't matter how many people you are responsible for feeding, not having this part of your life under control is an endless loop of wasted time, money, and mental well-being. No more.

Meal prep (aka meal planning) is a lifesaver for any busy person. When you start every week knowing exactly what's on the menu each night, dinner goes from a constant looming source of anxiety and insatiable devourer of time to a surgical strike.

You save money in so many meaningful ways: by keeping to a thought-out plan, shopping smart, not overbuying, and utilizing the ingredients you already have. Creating less waste is an additional benefit when you consider the average American throws away over one-third of the food they buy. By planning, your produce stays fresh and gets used, and you only purchase what you need for the week.

You save time, because you only go to the grocery once a week, don't waste time wondering what to make (and whether you have the ingredients to do so), and spend less time cooking and cleaning. Your level of stress *goes way down*.

Additionally, you wind up making smarter food choices—there is less mindless impulse eating because you've got a healthy meal at the ready.

So yes, meal prep really can help you save money and time and be happier and healthier. So, how do we make it happen?

The truth is you can't approach meal prep without first addressing organization. And I'll be the first to say it—organization can be a frigging nightmare of a task, especially when it comes to the kitchen.

How My Kitchen Got Its Groove Back

Your kitchen is not just about food. Yes, recipes are cooked, and meals are eaten there, but it's also the space in which the days with our families start and end, making the time spent cooking and eating part of a much larger fabric. The kitchen is a place where to-do reminders, held in place by quirky magnets or old pieces of frayed adhesive tape, punctuate the refrigerator door. It's the room where plans are made and homework is done. The kitchen table is where dreams are hatched and report cards reviewed, where bills are paid, pictures drawn, and board games played. There's a reason why politicians refer to the topics they use to appeal to voters as "kitchen table issues" or why the kitchen is the setting for so many of our meaningful childhood memories.

Put simply, the kitchen is where life happens. And even in the best of times, life gets messy. In every corner of the room, stuff inevitably accumulates—refrigerator produce, counter produce, spices, baking staples, garbage bags, gadgets, tools, pots, pans, that oversized food processor you use just twice a year that your estranged Uncle Ray said he selected himself (much to your surprise) off your wedding registry, canned goods, foil and plastic wrap, storage containers, and last, but not least, that thing that's been in your knife drawer since 2005, which has always been a mystery but you still keep in case you ever find out how to use it. Subsequently, it's also the only room in our homes that requires a frequent turnover of inventory. It's disturbing to me to think how many times in a single week I used to visit the supermarket.

Our kitchens tell the story of our lives: Among other things, they're a window into our health and wellness, our taste preferences, and our cultural backgrounds; an example of the routines in our lives (or lack thereof); and an indication of how particular we and/or our children can be about eating. Above all, if you are the one who's primarily responsible for

getting meals on the table, the kitchen serves as a constant reminder of how much we need to do, how good we are at doing it, and how thankless a job cooking can be, no matter what our skill levels are. (Think about it: Is there anything worse than visiting the home of a friend whose kitchen essentially screams, *I can cook, I'm organized, and if you think this is impressive, you should see the rest of my life!*?) None of us should feel like we require therapy just to take care of our family's basic needs, but why can it feel like that for so many of us?

When viewing the kitchen in the above light, it's easy to see why organizing it in a manner that puts you in control of it (rather than the other way around) and feeling confident in the space is fundamental to meal prep. The two go hand in hand. And the discovery of that connection is why I wanted to write this book.

Establishing Bona Fides (or, Laying Bare My Inner Marie Kondo)

When I was fifteen years old, I started modeling professionally, which meant that, for many years, the place I called home changed constantly. I lived all over the world in different apartments. It was a thrilling opportunity that I was blessed to experience, but it was also a chaotic existence that required me to be in a state of continuously creating and imposing my own order upon it. In the span of seven or so years, I must have lived in more than twenty-five apartments. Some had kitchens as small as a broom closet, others had fully equipped kitchens. Often, the apartments were furnished, which meant I was forced to use whatever unfamiliar kitchen setup had been left in place by the owner, and thus constantly needed to adapt my cooking style to my new environs.

Yet cooking for so long in unfamiliar surroundings with varying degrees of resources taught me an important lesson: Happiness can depend on how well you make your space work for

food lady. I had just had a child, and despite feeling unprepared, I was determined to find the healthiest and easiest way to feed him, and I shared my discoveries with a growing online audience. As time went on, I had more kids, and as those kids (and the kids of the Weelicious community) grew up, I then was labeled in the press and elsewhere with new sobriquets like *family food blogger, the school lunch chick,* and *smoothie girl.* However, if you follow Weelicious or have read any of my previous books, you might recall that I attended culinary school, and that I'm a lifelong obsessive collector and reader of cookbooks, all things that demand organization.

The Navy SEAL portion of my kitchen organization training began in culinary school and continued during my stints working in restaurants in New York and Los Angeles, where I was required to internalize the sacred art of *mise en place* (a French culinary term meaning to "put in place"). If your kitchen station wasn't in perfect order whenever one of your teachers or a chef walked by, you would be berated or given a slap on the wrist (sometimes literally), as anything less adversely impacts your ability to prepare foods in an efficient manner. Turns out, running a home kitchen isn't so different from running a restaurant kitchen, and in more ways than you might imagine.

Similarly, walls full of cookbooks can quickly transform into a muddled blur of recipes and techniques, which is why I fill them with sticky notes and earmark the pages, so I remember to cook the things that appeal to me most, then I annotate the recipes with my thoughts and customizations after cooking them for future use. Having an

you. I discovered early on that when my kitchen wasn't organized to serve the demands of my lifestyle, I carried the effects of that chaos with me, and so those years formed the foundation of how I learned to make my kitchen accommodate my way of life, and not the other way around. Still, the challenges of kitchen organization only seemed to multiply as I got older, and those skills I honed early in life have served me, and in turn, my family.

When I started my company Weelicious more than fifteen years ago, I was referred to as the *baby*

easy-to-reference library of curated family-friendly recipes always available at your fingertips is also one of the reasons I created Weelicious in the first place. Cooking for a family is hard enough.

As my family has grown, I've increasingly become a consumer of organizational guides as well, not just because a family of five accumulates a lot of crap over time, but because I discovered that I was able to incorporate and adapt many of the general organizational principles I found in them to my kitchen meal prep routine. It was at first an unintentional—and somewhat unconscious—marriage between the two disciplines on my part, since meal prep is something that I've been doing religiously for so long. Reading the general household strategies of organizational experts, I began drawing specific connections between some of what they detailed and the meal prep systems I'd learned and developed over time. For example, I keep my clothing ordered by color and season, so when I'm looking for, say, a pair of white pants, I waste no time finding them. However, I'd never collected all of that knowledge into a personal meal prep system—at least not consciously—until the pandemic hit and I realized that so many people were struggling with issues that my strategies could help address.

You can take control and feel comfortable and confident in your cooking space, even if you are in a tiny galley kitchen, outfitted with nothing but the basics. *You can make magic.* All you need is the how, and I'm here to share what I've learned.

Necessity Is the Mother of (Re)Invention

Our lives changed dramatically over the past few years. As with so many aspects of our lifestyles, the COVID-19 pandemic forced us all to reexamine our lives, viewing acts we once took for granted—such as eating out or the simple task of running into the grocery to grab a few last-minute items—in an entirely different light. In this new normal, everyday activities suddenly transformed into forbidden luxuries.

Likewise, lockdowns illuminated the significance of things that we barely thought about or had neglected completely, such as the experience of cooking at home. Being confined to our abodes for months on end underscored the importance of feeding your family, not just from a nutritional standpoint, but as a core value—bringing families together, even during the most difficult of times. No matter how rough the quarantine lifestyle was for families, I think many would agree that one of its few blessings was that we shared meals together, sometimes even virtually, more regularly than ever. A global tragedy transformed—mostly for the better—the way that people cook, and in turn solidified bonds between family members. As life slowly started to return to what we used to consider normal, numerous parents remarked to me that they want to remain proactive about maintaining the family meal.

That being said, the degree of pleasantness (or unpleasantness, depending on who you ask) experienced by people having to cook almost every meal likely had a great deal to do with how organized they were and, unbeknownst to them, how set up for success (or failure) each person was. No matter our skill level in the kitchen, many of us have a positive connection to food, and view cooking not just as a means to sustenance, but as a way of bringing the family together and making memories. Nevertheless, many of us experience frustration in the kitchen, either because we believe we can't cook, or because the whole process simply feels overwhelming at the end of a long day, causing additional stress. Even the simplest of family meals can result in tears, hurt feelings, or uttering expletives that would make even the most die-hard New Yorker blush. Worse, bad cooking experiences can lead to many of us giving up entirely on home cooking and abandoning any hope of accomplishing a task that should be realistic and enjoyable for all of us, no matter how busy we may be.

Success in the kitchen comes down to two things in my view: a **well-organized space** and **meal prep**. And as I stated at the outset, the two are intrinsically connected. Any accomplished chef or home cook will tell you that organization, more so than any ingredient, is the most important skill any home cook can possess. You might be blessed with an abundance of culinary dexterity, but if you don't have an organized system behind it, consistently good results will elude you. The more organized you are, the better your outcomes will be, from taste (I'm not kidding when I say that you and your diners will be able to taste it in the food), to getting a meal on the table on time. Poor organization can take what should be a joyful experience, and instead make you lose your appetite.

Conversely, someone with the most rudimentary of cooking skills will have uniformly positive outcomes if their kitchen is organized to support and scaffold them. Every second wasted looking for a tool, rummaging through a chaotic pantry, or searching in cluttered drawers is not just annoying; it's time taken away from the food. Equally important, it's time wasted that could have better been spent with family or relaxing by yourself while everything is cooking. Being organized in the kitchen saves time, money, and, above all, your sanity. It creates an atmosphere of calm and confidence while leaving room for you and your family to make memories. You don't have to think about anything other than what you are cooking and for whom you're cooking.

However, even for those of us who are competent cooks, the basic strategies of efficient kitchen organization are not common knowledge and are not always intuitive.

Kitchen Zen

While people may not be completely conscious of the connection between organization and meal planning, or instinctively know how to integrate the two, they do have some innate appreciation for it and crave it. "Refrigerator porn" is not just an amusing term. Whenever I post an organization photo of any part of my kitchen to the Weelicious Instagram account, I receive endless questions from people in the comment section asking how they can get their pantry/refrigerator/freezer/drawers to look the same way. They're often followed by "What tools do I need?" or "What recipes or ingredients can I turn into a bunch of meals that last the week?" and so forth.

In this busy, overwhelming, and oftentimes crazy world, we're all looking for a bit of zen wherever we can find it. We are trying to claw back as much time as possible to spend on the things that matter most to us. Between serving up to three meals a day, seven days a week (your math is correct, that's twenty-one meals a week), plus endless snacks, parents can face a revolving door of hungry, occasionally irritable, diners wanting and needing their food fast.

No matter the size of your kitchen, it can be organized in a manner that best serves the way you like to cook, reduces stress, and creates more pleasure. While reading this book, I invite you to close your eyes and visualize the kitchen you want, along with all of its potential. It's one hundred percent achievable and requires less effort or money than you may think. And once you get a streamlined system in place that works for you, it's not difficult to maintain. Clutter triggers anxiety, which makes you want to bolt from your cooking space, instead of enjoying your time there. The phrase "less is more" has never been more accurate than in your dream kitchen. When you venture into your kitchen, you should feel calm and confident. My goal for you is to know how to maximize your kitchen, no matter its size, to its fullest. Together we're going to make it happen, because it is attainable. So, where to start?

A Quick Note About How to Get the Most Out of This Book

To help you create a meal prep system that will serve you for years to come, I've organized this book into four sections. The sections—**PURGE**, **ORGANIZE**, **PREP**, and **EXECUTE**—are meant to be followed in order.

That may seem daunting, but it's much simpler than it sounds. The analogy I like to use is: Think about your desire to make meal prep your bitch as if it's a dream of yours to go to space—right now, both goals might seem pretty far-fetched. In the case of your space dream, you need a rocket—usually comprised of a couple of stages—powerful enough to overcome Earth's gravitational pull and take you to the stars. Once one of those stages has burned through its fuel capacity, it's no longer necessary—it's dead weight—and it separates from the rocket. Then the remaining stages are spent and released, and there you are, floating among the stars, dream accomplished.

Now, let's apply that idea to how to use this book to deliver you to space, or rather the meal prep promised land. In this case, gravity is everything currently preventing you from dominating meal prep (e.g., limited time, motivation, techniques). The rocket is this book and the "stages" of the book are the first two sections, PURGE and ORGANIZE. Once you get through them and get your organizational foundation in place, those two stages of the rocket fall away. You're more or less done with them for good. They (and you) have done the hard work so all you need focus on going forward is maintaining the well-being of your environment (what I call the PREP section) and you, now rocking out in deep space as you take control of mealtime (the EXECUTE section), which, much like space travel, offers its own sense of weightlessness.

STAGE
1

Purge

YOU CAN'T build a house without a good foundation and, as I said earlier, to fully realize the magical benefits of meal prep you must create a structure that supports your goals, otherwise you won't have a meal system that endures. I didn't exit the womb as an organization freak. My room was messy as a kid (to which my mother will happily attest). An overzealous eight-year-old aspiring chef, I left an endless trail of disorder in our kitchen. Throughout my teens, the back of my little car looked like a family of five was living in it. In the ensuing years, especially now as a mother caring for a houseful of people, I've learned key strategies to keep our home—especially our kitchen, given that it is easily the most heavily trafficked room in our house—in order.

The goal of this first PURGE section, as well as the following ORGANIZE section, is to transform your kitchen into a place where your family enjoys spending time. Once you've worked through these parts of the book, not only will you be set up to crush meal prep, you'll be able to move around your cooking space easily without pots and pans clattering out of cabinets or the need to sift through cluttered drawers full of cooking tools whose basic function is unclear. We'll go through what you need and what's OK to toss in order to create a calm and soothing space.

Time Is on Your Side

Step one is to set aside at least a day or two to clear out your space. That may sound like a lot of time, but remember that the ease of maintaining this meal prep system rests on this foundational work. Once you're done with the initial purge, this stage of the meal prep rocket more or less falls away for good. The work you put in now pays off, so err on the side of giving yourself more time to work on it than less. If you have kids and can make some time during school hours when no one is around, that's an ideal environment to operate in. Personally, I prefer the

weekend, when I have fewer distractions and can get in my favorite cozy sweats, put on some inspiring tunes or a podcast I'm behind on, and get to work.

Road Map: Purge Sub-Stages
I. REMOVE
II. ASSESS
III. EDIT
IV. CLEAN

I. REMOVE

When you think of "spring cleaning," maybe you associate it with shedding and donating clothes from your closet that you no longer wear. Bring that same mindset to this kitchen purge process. For some, this may feel like an overwhelming task, but stick with me and have the courage to rip off the Band-Aid because the entire journey to mealtime happiness begins with—and depends upon—this step.

When you make organize your kitchen properly, you're giving your brain a rest from the clutter (both mental and physical) that impairs you from being the best chef you can be. No matter your kitchen's size, you need to start with a clean slate, which means removing every item, be it an ingredient or cookware, from every drawer, rack, cabinet, or storage area. You need to see and understand what you have before you can determine what you really need.

Do *not* remove everything stored in your kitchen all at once. Instead, divide your kitchen into digestible pieces so that you can focus on the task at hand and not become overwhelmed. I suggest breaking the room up into zones, both big and small (e.g., refrigerator, freezer, pantry, utensil drawer, etc.), and then, depending on the size of your zone (a zone can be as big as your refrigerator to as small as a knife drawer), break them up even further (e.g., if you are working on the fridge, remove items one shelf at a time). Take whatever approach you think will work best for you. Make sure that you give yourself a large enough area in which to place all the items you are removing, as the goal is to remove everything. This part may feel like you're creating an even bigger mess, but it's the only way to really see what you've got (often you'll find a few forgotten treasures, which makes it a wee bit exciting too). To make the next steps of the process a bit easier, I recommend that as you are emptying each section, if you discover compatible items that were living separately when you removed them, group them in your workspace (e.g., if you have several bottles of hot sauces, keep them together).

In case you need some assistance designating your zones, here's a sample breakdown:

✦ Refrigerator
✦ Freezer
✦ Pantry
✦ Pots/pans/cookware
✦ Spices
✦ Utensils
✦ Linens (tea towels, napkins, cleaning cloths)
✦ Storage containers
✦ Kitchen tools
✦ Small appliances
✦ Countertop

Start wherever you prefer; I recommend starting with something big like the fridge or pantry to get it out of the way and experience the process fully. Once you finish all of the steps in this section for a zone, jump ahead to the next section, ORGANIZE, and create your new space (see page 24). As you'll see, many of my organization tips can be applied anywhere in your kitchen; however, in the next chapter, I also give specific ideas for each individual zone.

II. ASSESS

Now that you have pulled out everything for a particular zone, it's time to investigate what you have.

The first thing you should do (if you haven't already done so during the REMOVE stage) is separate everything into categories (e.g., for food, I mean sauces, dressings, grains, canned goods, etc., and for cookware, I mean pots, pans, spatulas, baking dishes, etc.). If the zone you are working on involves food, check expiration dates and toss anything past its prime (remember to recycle when possible!).

At this point, you may be surprised to see how much you have of one thing or how little of another (in the case of the latter, I've got suggestions on what you need for a well-functioning kitchen at the end of this section). I've been completely surprised on occasion to discover I have multiple Dijon mustards stored in my pantry or to find that the mesh in my strainer has ripped since I used it last.

III. EDIT

Time to start deciding what stays . . . and what goes. This is where the rubber meets the road.

We All Need a Bestie Now and Then

Over the years, I've worked with and spoken to organizational experts and one of the best tips I've learned from them for getting through this next part of the process is to have a friend, or someone impartial you know, come over for a few hours to work with you. This person need not have any organizational experience, only an understanding of their role to be a practitioner of tough love and make sure at the end of the day there's at least one bin or garbage bag packed full of items, ready to leave your space. If you feel confident that you can go through this process on your own, the more power to you, but in my experience, someone who's patient enough to help go through each and every drawer and cabinet, keep you honest as to why you really don't need to hold on to that lobster claw cracker you've never

used, and then hold you accountable to donate or toss the things you really don't need has been invaluable in my own journey.

If you don't like the idea of having a friend or loved one witness the messy agony of purging your pantry and cupboards, there are endless organizational experts who are truly worth the money and then some. They'll support you through the process, and in the long run, from a time and effort standpoint, hiring them may be an even more efficient way to get it all done.

Purging can definitely be a painful experience for some ("Sure the mesh is broken, but that was my Aunt Myrna's favorite flour sifter"). As much as you may treasure a kitchen tool given to you by a loved one and need to hold on to it for posterity, the space it takes up in your kitchen may outweigh its sentimental value. If it is an item of quality or durability and you use it, by all means keep it, but remember that ultimately, parting with clutter is incredibly liberating. Out of all of the kitchen items I've donated over the years, there's only one item I

wish I had held on to. (And just so you can get it out of your head, it was a tortilla press. And no, you don't need one!)

The Power of Goodbye

Many of us, when confronted with something we own, even when we forgot we even owned it, have a reflexive "you never know when I might need it" response. That's how we end up with cabinets that we could not begin to list the contents of and drawers packed so tight (with who knows what) that we have to pry them open just to get the one thing we actually need. Much like the sentimental rationales we create for not parting with clothing we never wear, when it comes to getting rid of kitchen stuff, we suddenly become culinary Boy Scouts—"We never use those souvenir sake glasses, but maybe someday we'll have that sushi soiree we've thought about for a decade and those glasses will be perfect!". Friend, I've been there. You'll never have that sushi party, and if you do, buy a new set for the occasion.

Each of us is going to be different when it comes to determining what's useful, special, or necessary, so don't overthink it or feel like you're not doing it right or well enough. Pick out the tools you can't live without or that make you a strong cook in the kitchen and put those in one pile ("**Keep**"). Next, select the items that you use less frequently and place them in a second pile. Finally, create a third pile that consists of tools and gadgets you've rarely used or which are broken or not working well ("**Goodbye**," more on that later). A note on the second pile: these are tools you're unsure of for the moment but must relegate to the Keep or Goodbye piles before moving onto the ORGANIZE stage (Keep reading for tips to help you with those decisions).

Kitchen Tools That Earn Their Keep

At one time or another I've owned or used just about every small kitchen tool you can imagine. My grandparents used to watch QVC and HSN constantly, and knowing I loved cooking from an early age, bought me almost every culinary-related thing advertised, from a pancake batter dispenser to an onion chopper to a corn stripper. Today, my favorite kitchen tools are made for their unique design, usefulness, and durability.

Here is a list of my must-have kitchen tools. If you own items not on this list, consider whether you really need them.

Sheet pan: One of my go-to cooking methods is lining a sheet pan with parchment paper (hello easy nonstick cleanup!), tossing on a variety of proteins and veggies with herbs and spices, and roasting them at a high heat until tender inside and crispy outside. Shrimp, chicken, sausage, salmon, tofu, and most vegetables marry beautifully when roasted together on a sheet pan.

Box grater: A tool that earns its space in my drawer because it has both practical and sentimental value. I've had the same box grater since I was eighteen years old and it's still a workhorse. I use it for grating cheese, fresh ginger and turmeric, and even thin strips of zucchini.

Cutting boards: BPA-free, dishwasher-safe cutting boards (one small, one large) for preparing meat, poultry, and fish, and one larger wood or bamboo cutting board that can be hand washed for fruits and vegetables.

Can opener: A well-made hand crank opener will last you a lifetime.

Colander: For draining pasta and washing produce and salad greens, I highly recommend using metal colanders, as I try and reduce my use of plastic and I don't like draining boiling pasta water through plastic.

Hand mandolin: For slicing cucumbers, carrots, and radishes for salad; potatoes to make potato chips; ribbons of zucchini for a pasta dish; and anything else you want thinly sliced. Look for one that allows you to adjust the thickness of the slice and has a safety guard.

Instant-Read thermometer: To ensure you don't under- or overcook meats and poultry.

Juicer: I have a sturdy hand juicer that works like magic for lemons, limes, oranges, and other citrus. If you enjoy making juices or lemonade, which require more work, there are plenty of reasonably priced electric juicers.

Kitchen shears: For everything from trimming or cutting chicken into chunks (avoids the need for a cutting board), cutting vegetables, snipping herbs, opening packages, and much more, I often refer to this tool as my best friend in the kitchen.

Knives: A fancy set is nice, but not necessary to create killer meals. I have quite an extensive collection, but that is purely related to my profession. You can get excellent results with just an 8- or 10-inch (20 to 25 cm) chef's knife, 3½-inch (9 cm) paring knife, and 8- to 12-inch (20 to 30.5 cm) serrated knife.

Measuring cups: A ¼, ⅓, ½, and 1 cup set for dry measuring. I recommend a good steel set, which will last forever and can safely go in the dishwasher. A 2- or 4-cup Pyrex liquid measure is also essential.

Measuring spoons: A ⅛, ¼, ½, and 1 teaspoon plus 1 tablespoon set. Again, stick to metal over plastic for cleaning and longevity purposes.

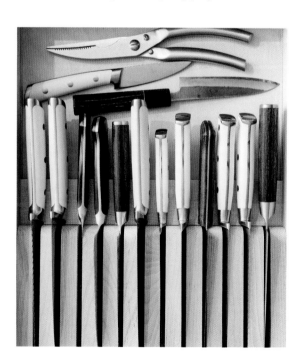

Meat mallet: For pounding chicken and meats to make the perfect scallopini. Also good for crushing nuts, or to brandish menacingly at your kids when they aren't listening to you. (I'm kidding about that last one—just making sure you're paying attention.)

Potato masher: For mashing potatoes, of course, but equally great for making homemade applesauce and celery root mash too!

Rolling pin: A must for roll-out cookies and other types of dough.

Silicone spatulas: The hands-down winner when it comes to making sure you get every last drop of batter from a mixing bowl, honey from a measuring cup, or smoothie from your blender, or for extracting all of the mustard, nut butter, or jam from a jar. (You'll be shocked when you see how much you've been tossing out over the years in those supposedly empty containers.) Get a set of small and large ones.

Soup ladle: This one is pretty obvious.

Tongs: Small and large for serving salad and vegetables, turning meat while cooking, and more. I primarily use stainless ones for durability and food safety. The plastic-tipped ones melt in high heat. If

you want a pair of those, find one with heat-resistant, food-grade silicone.

Vegetable peeler: A sharp one, preferably with a silicone handle, which makes peeling faster, easier, and less likely to waste food. The old-fashioned metal ones always hurt my hand when I do a lot of peeling. Note: I'm not a fan of the T-shaped peelers with the blade positioned perpendicular to the handle. I want the blade to be like an extension of my arm.

Wire whisk: Small and large for whisking sauces and batter.

Wooden spoons and flat-edge turners: Without exaggeration, I use these every day.

Thinking Outside of the Box: Nifty Tool Hacks and How to Turn Single-Purpose Gadgets into Multi-Use Ones

Madison Avenue would have you believe that no kitchen is complete without a 3-in-1 Avocado Peeler/Pitter/Cuber, and while every now and then I see something that seems really useful, I find the majority of these tools to be clever, yes, but absolutely unnecessary. They save neither time nor effort, and you have to find a place to store them. Ultimately, you're wasting your money.

✦ Don't have a rolling pin? Use an empty wine bottle (remove the label).

✦ Ice cream scoops come in different sizes and can do way more than just serve ice cream. Use them to portion cookie dough, make perfectly round meatballs, or to portion muffin batter into tins.

✦ In addition to prepping your morning beans, use your coffee grinder to chop herbs and spices and to turn toasted bread into breadcrumbs. If grinding spices or herbs, be sure to thoroughly clean the grinder afterward, so you don't unintentionally flavor your next cup of coffee.

✦ Ice cube trays can be used to make wine, lemonade, or coffee cubes to keep these

inside you need one STAT. Think perfectly cooked chicken, vegetables, and fish; crispy quesadillas; expertly reheated pizza; and healthy french fries, as well as a healthier way to heat prepared foods from your freezer that you want to eat fast while still getting all the crispiness frying provides. Another bonus? Air fryers are easy to clean. This is coming from someone who truly hates doing dishes.

Multi-cooker: Electric pressure cookers, Instant Pots, slow cookers, and sous vides are all brilliant cooking tools, but if you want one of each, you better have the space to store them. A slow cooker may seem contrary to the idea of getting meals on the table fast, but it's a lifesaver, requiring little effort and delivering lots of flavor. If you love braised meats, stews, soups, or overnight oatmeal, this appliance is for you. Simply dump the recipe ingredients into the pot, turn it on, leave for work, and return hours later to find dinner ready. If speed is your need, pressure cookers can cook beans and other foods that normally require more time in a mere fraction of it. Instant Pots and sous vides each have differing cooking specialties (and devoted fans too). Multi-cookers, depending on the brand, perform a combination of these (if not all) functions but occupy the space of just one small appliance. I have a slow cooker and a pressure cooker, however I now use my multi-cooker to cook dried beans, grains, pulses, and tougher cuts of meat that generally have longer cook times.

Blender: Making the decision to buy a strong/high-speed blender will be one of your best kitchen investments in the long run. We use our blender every single day to make smoothies, nice cream (aka healthy ice cream), pureed soups, vinaigrettes, and more. There are endless models on the market, so ask a friend, read reviews, or send me a DM, and I'll make a suggestion!

Don't Worry, You're Not Creating an Island of Lost Toys

Even after considering what really is truly essential in your kitchen, deciding to put something into pile number three, *the goodbye pile*, can cause many

beverages cold without diluting them; keep herbs fresh (fill compartments with herbs, cover with water, and freeze); and freeze smaller portions of purees, sauces, or homemade broth or stock to use in future recipes as needed.

Keep Your Small Kitchen Appliance Game Tight

Review your appliances and consider which are all-stars and which aren't pulling their weight. If you want to maximize time-saving, and minimize expenditure of effort, these are the ones I recommend.

Air fryer: My love for my air fryer knows no bounds. So great is it, in fact, that *I own two*. You can cook everything you can cook in your oven in it (and more), without the need to preheat. Cooking food in an air fryer cuts the cooking time by as much as half, removes much of the added fat, and concentrates the flavors in whatever you're cooking. And if you love foods that are crispy on the outside and tender

of us stress, leaving us to punt those items into pile two, where they will remain untouched for four more years, until you do this dance over again.

Here are a few rules you can set up beforehand to help you get past falling into that trap: 1) If you haven't used an item within eighteen to twenty-four months, it goes. 2) If an item won't cost you more than 20 minutes or $20 to replace, it goes.

"Goes" means toss it, donate it, or give it to a friend (more about that process shortly)—after which, you don't think about it anymore. It's the easiest way to clear space in your drawers, cupboards, and pantry as well as feel good that you are making those unused tools available to those who will really use them.

Need guilt-free strategies for getting unwanted kitchenware out of your house? Here are a few ideas:

Donate: Whether you choose the Goodwill, a local shelter, or other resource, you can receive a tax deduction and feel better that your goods are going to those who need them most. Also, the Freecycle website (freecycle.org) is a great nonprofit resource where you can list items you want to give away to others in your community, who are responsible for picking them up.

Sell: There are endless resources like local newsletters, Facebook Marketplace, eBay, Craigslist, and more where you can sell small kitchen appliances, cookbooks, or even boxes full of tools. Yard sales are also a fun way to purge and put cash in your pocket.

Recycle: If the first two options aren't possible, make sure you recycle so your stuff doesn't end up in a landfill. If you have broken small electronic appliances, look online for your local options for recycling e-waste. There are often plenty of options you can feel good about using.

IV. CLEAN

The hardest part is done. Before moving onto the ORGANIZE stage, I strongly suggest cleaning your emptied zone out. Personally, I need to see that the environment is physically clean before anything goes back into it.

Unless you're a neat freak, I'd wager that, say, your silverware drawer, or the cabinet with your pots and pans, hasn't been cleared out, given a good spray, and wiped down in months—most likely years. Don't feel guilty about it. None of us have time for that, however now we have a chance to make it look and feel spick-and-span. When it comes to cleaning products, I stick with all-natural products from companies committed to avoiding harmful or toxic chemicals. Seventh Generation, Grove Co., Mrs. Meyers, and Branch Basics are among a few I like. Or save money using one of my favorite cleaning hacks: Mix equal parts water and distilled white vinegar in a spray bottle and, if desired, add some lemon, grapefruit, or orange peel for scent. It is inexpensive and excellent for cleaning everything in your kitchen from surfaces to crusty pots and pans.

Think about this part as your stuff moving into a beautiful, new home. Don't just focus on shelves and such—make the whole kitchen feel brand new. If the inside of your cabinets look scratched and dingy, consider adding fresh shelf liners. If there are scuffs on the walls and cabinets, get those now too. Sometimes you encounter the particularly hard-to-remove stain or mold, and in those situations when you've exhausted trying to do it in an earth-friendly way, other methods are required. I've used Mr. Clean sponges to remove markers, crayons, footprints (yes, footprints on my walls), and much more. These pads are magical, especially if you've got white walls or cabinets. I recommend investing in a stack of them. And finally, if you have been putting off updating your art, window treatments, or other decorations; slapping on a fresh coat of paint; or doing any other minor, inexpensive cosmetic fixes in your kitchen, there's no time like the present.

Now it's time to look at your blank slate of a zone and figure out how to populate it in a clutter-free, easy-to-use way.

Organize

PEPPERS

STRAWBERRIES

RADISHES

APPLES

PINK PINEAPPLE

POMEGRANATE

RASPBERRY

STRAWBERRY

KUMQUAT

PEPPERS

La Croix

BOK CHOY

LETTUCE

GARLIC

THIS PART is kinda fun, especially if you feel a bit beaten up by Stage 1. Now is when you get to create the system that will be the underpinning of your meal prep magic.

PASTA

Mise en Place Is Just a Fancy Way of Saying "Uncomplicate Your Shit": Choosing Things You Need Close By vs. the Things You Don't

In culinary school, one of the first things we were taught is the critical importance of *mise en place*, a French culinary term for having everything in its place. Culinary schools are in the business of turning out professional chefs. The word "business" is important here, because while a chef can create a menu of the most brilliant creations, none of that matters if her kitchen cannot turn it out hour after hour, night after night, year after year, with near-perfect consistency. That means every individual in the kitchen, from the sous chef, to the line cooks, to the expediter, to the dishwasher must perform with almost robotic-like accuracy. There can be no weak link. A restaurant succeeds or fails based on the speed, talent, and precision of its kitchen team. Every line cook's job, no matter what their station (salads, grill, pastry, etc.) depends on having perfect mise en place—every ingredient and tool prepped within reach so that the cook need think about nothing but the food.

Time spent stopping to peel something or reach for a knife is additional time your diners have to wait to get their food, and it affects the flow of the entire kitchen organism. I once watched an episode of an Anthony Bourdain (I miss him so) show where he was spotlighting a sushi master who talked about how his prior career as a boxer trained him to be a better chef. Every single movement the boxer makes has purpose and requires an expense of energy; therefore, every movement is precious. This chef carried himself like a boxer when making

sushi, avoiding any wasted movement. Being a chef requires intense focus and stamina—all of which must go into the food.

While some might say the degree of difficulty required to feed your family every night pales in comparison to working in a professional kitchen, all I can say is this: I've done both jobs, and neither is a walk in the park, but applying the lessons I learned in professional kitchens about mise en place to being a home cook have made that job a heck of a lot easier.

To help manage this process, I suggest separating your kitchen into zones like the ones we discussed on page 17 (which are again listed in the pages to follow) and addressing each one at a time. As a general principle, when beginning to organize a zone, consider first how you want to interact with the area. Going forward, let that influence the organizational decisions you make to optimize it. For example, are there cooking tools you use frequently but normally live beyond arm's reach? Conversely, is there a drawer in your prep space containing items you rarely touch? Similarly, in your fridge or pantry, are there ingredients you use and replace regularly that live obscured behind a bunch of lesser-used items or, worse, ingredients you forgot you had even owned even though they are located prominently? Your preferred way of operating in the kitchen should dictate where you put things, not the other way around. Consider swapping the location of the contents in certain drawers and cabinets so that when you're cooking, you're not crossing the kitchen to grab a tool that should be right there. Correcting these seemingly negligible inconveniences now will add up to major time- and effort-savings in the future.

Zone-Specific Organization Tips

Refrigerator: No matter how many shelves you have, your fridge will complicate organizing it exactly the way you want. That is where bins and other fridge organization aids can be used to meet your needs. Group items by category, and arrange them by prioritizing the foods you use most. This tip may seem obvious, but I find it to be an oft overlooked one. In my fridge, the foods we eat most often are placed in the main part of the fridge and lesser-used foods and condiments sit either on the shelves attached to our refrigerator door or in the lowest regions of the main part. For me, that means milks, yogurts, and specialty drinks go on the top shelf; eggs, dips (school lunch staples like hummus, olive tapenade, etc.), pickles, olives, krauts, and leftovers on the second shelf; fruits, such as seasonal berries and apples, are situated on the third shelf (see page 39 for stay-fresh storage tips); beverages and large, see-through, food-safe plastic bins labeled with their contents' names—foods we eat most like avocados—on the fourth shelf; meats, cold cuts, cheeses, and dog food on the fifth shelf; and the remaining produce in the crisper. Having separate labeled containers helps ensure you don't forget about them and can always locate them. When you buy new foods, if you still have some of the same food already remaining in the fridge, store the newer item behind

the older one to ensure you use the oldest first. Our fridges may be configured differently, so you may not be able to replicate my system exactly, but the principles remain the same.

Freezer: I view my freezer as my backstop, an ace in the hole when I'm too busy to prepare a meal from scratch or am out of leftovers from the previous night. Here, I can always be sure there are pre-prepared, ready-to-eat meals that need only be heated up; a reserve of fruits and veggies that can always be employed on a moment's notice for a smoothie or healthy side dish; and the long-term storage of staple ingredients. For example, as soon as I buy nuts, seeds, and whole grains like quinoa, wheat berries, or millet (all things that tend to go rancid), I transfer them from their packages to glass jars (so I can easily see their contents) and put them in the freezer. Similar to how I organize my refrigerator, I separate foods into categories, giving the most oft-used ingredients places of prominence. If you're anything like me, you'll take great care setting aside what is my favorite section, the one for ice cream and popsicles.

Pantry: Have you ever been excited to make a recipe, and know you have all the ingredients because you saw them in the pantry, only to later discover someone used virtually all of an ingredient and replaced the box on the shelf as if it were full? How about finding opened bags of pasta, cereal, pretzels, rice, and everything in between, stuffed into the nether regions of your pantry? These are among my top pet peeves. And when those items also turn out to be stale . . . well, you better hope you're not within earshot of me when that happens.

Solution? As soon as I get home from the grocery, I recycle the packaging and transfer the contents into airtight, transparent glass containers to keep my food fresher longer. Not only does it allow me to see what I have (and how much of it), it inspires me to cook with it. It also makes my pantry look pleasing to the eye. Remember that sense of zen we talked about earlier? Yup, a simple container change

can help guarantee that feeling. I prefer using a variety of sizes of mason jars as they are inexpensive, airtight, and look great.

It's not only the glass containers that reduce the visual clutter of shelves stocked with packaging of various sizes and colors. Equipping your pantry with lazy Susans, stackable containers, and/or tiered shelving will allow you to maximize your cubic footage, and create zones within zones. I micro focus, establishing sections for sweet snacks, salty snacks, hot sauces, pastas, rice, and more, so now I always know exactly what I've got on hand and exactly where to find it.

Cookware/pots/pans: Pots and pans can be stored in a variety of ways depending on the amount of space you have available. If you have a deep cabinet that can accomodate a lazy Susan-type shelf, that is ideal for stacking your cookware, placing smaller pots and pans with their lids on one shelf and larger ones on another. I actually keep all my lids separate in a convenient standing divider, which allows me to maximize pot and pan storage space without worrying about lids. Pegboards (see page 37) or hanging racks are other good ways to keep pots and pans, reserving cabinet storage for food or glassware.

Spices: Having a solid collection of spices can transform otherwise ordinary meals into extraordinary ones, but they can be a time suck if you can't easily find what you need when you need it. Being able to see them is key. Depending on your preference or available space, there are a number of efficient, and also aesthetically pleasing, ways to store your spices, from using tiered storage, to a rack mounted inside a cabinet or pantry door, to laying the bottles on their side, label up, in a drawer. I suggest alphabetizing them like they do in the supermarket, which makes navigation effortless (for this reason, I don't like lazy Susans for spices as it's harder to maintain this way).

If you are like me and get tweaked looking at a collection of randomly sized and labeled bottles, you can either try to buy your spices from just one high-quality spice company (such as Simply Organic, McCormick, the Spice House, Penzeys, or Oaktown Spice Shop, to name a few). Another option is to purchase smaller amounts of spices you use less frequently at bulk bin stores or half-size bottles at your local grocery or online. That can be challenging, especially if you already have a good spice collection, so you can purchase inexpensive sets of small, air-tight glass bottles, some of which come with pre-printed labels, to transfer your spices into (from brands like Spice It Your Way, the Bottle Store, the Container Store, or Crate and Barrel). While it takes a bit of effort at the outset, it results in an organization system that's pretty enough to be displayed. Additionally, as most of the bottles that brands package their spices in are not wide enough to fit a measuring spoon into, I like that the mouths of the bottles I have allow for me to fit a tablespoon into them and neatly remove the precise amount.

Utensils: I won't go into everyday cutlery, as a drawer utensil organizer is likely the one thing everyone has in their kitchen; however, large jars near the range or between dividers in deep drawers are handy for other utensils used for cooking or serving.

Knives: A close cousin to utensils, I broke this one out because knives are specialized tools that deserve dedicated space, and because of their relative size and your safety needs, they have several storage options. Aside from countertop knife blocks, which look nice and can store even a large number of knives, there are also wall-mounted magnetic options that allow you to simply "hang" your knife in a convenient location. Given my profession, I have a lot of knives—far too many to store in a block on the counter or clutter on a magnetic wall strip without being an eyesore—so I keep them in a deep drawer outfitted with two slotted knife trays. It's very clean and efficient, especially considering that I have knives of greatly varying lengths.

Linens (potholders, tea towels, cloth napkins): Remember going to the grocery in the beginning of the pandemic and seeing the paper product aisles bare? I've always tried to keep our paper towel usage to a minimum, but even more so in the ensuing years. Cloth towels are a lifesaver in the kitchen, for wiping off your hands to drying produce, placing a slightly damp one under a cutting board to prevent it from sliding, wiping down counter tops, and wrapping up to use as an oven mitt. The best part is the more you wash them, the softer they get, making them easier to roll or fold. I recommend using them with abandon, and for tasks you might have considered a paper towel for. Invest in an inexpensive set of cotton kitchen towels and store them in a dedicated drawer closest to where you prep in the kitchen, so they are easy to grab as you cook and clean. If you don't have enough drawer space, you can keep your supply stacked in a basket or container under the sink. Napkins and potholders can be kept in the same place if you have space, or divide them, keeping napkins near the place you eat most and potholders close to the oven.

Small appliances: Considering how much valuable space they often take up, the name "small appliance" can feel misleading. Especially if you are working with a constrained amount of available storage space, figuring out how to organize your small appliances can be a frustrating task. It obviously depends on the size of your kitchen and available shelf space, but even if you're blessed with ample counters, I recommend keeping no more than two or three of your most used small appliances on the kitchen counter. It may require slightly more effort to retrieve an appliance from a closet or cabinet (or even a basement!), but unless it's something you're using daily, I consider the benefit of uncluttered counter space to be a worthwhile trade-off. For my family, it's the blender, air fryer, and toaster that have earned prime countertop real estate. My less heavily used small kitchen appliances—multi-cooker, dehydrator, standing mixer, and more—are grouped together on a shelf at the top of my pantry.

Kitchen tools: Given the variety of tools you may have, it doesn't take long for constant use to result in your tool drawers looking more like a tangle of plastic, stainless steel, and silicone. As with food storage, organize and store kitchen tools by category and frequency of use. As drawer depths, lengths, and heights often vary greatly from home to home, modular, stackable, and changeable dividers can make all the difference, but don't spend your money on buying them (or effort on making your own) until you know exactly what you need.

Storage containers: Nine out of ten times I have leftovers from dinner. As much as I love a fresh-cooked meal, leftovers are my jam. The flavors meld more, and bonus: You have an easy grab-and-go meal for later in the week. I recommend having a range of storage containers and an organized way of keeping them until ready to use.

For those of us that have innocently collected a motley crew of plastic Tupperware—you know the ones I mean, with stains and missing lids—right now, I want you to stop and consider recycling them (see below for one type of plastic container I do hold on to—deli containers). Of course, plastic containers (as long as they are BPA-free) are OK for storing dried

Another great glass storage idea is mason jars. They're incredibly affordable, come in a variety of shapes and sizes, and like all glass are dishwasher safe. Some of my favorite brands are Rubbermaid, Wean Green, Pyrex, Glasslock, and PrepNaturals.

I love cooking for friends and always keep a secret stash of plastic deli containers tucked away in the pantry for those times when I want to gift food or send guests home with leftovers. Tracking down lent glassware is no fun, so having an assortment of containers you are happy to never see again comes in extremely handy. We don't do much takeout, so I buy an inexpensive set at Smart and Final, but if you get food that comes in a great reusable container (you'll know it when you see it), wash it well and set it aside.

Streamlining is key: I have one drawer in which I keep all of my storage containers and lids. Twice a year I go through them to make sure every bottom has a top, discarding any without a mate. The rule of thumb is only to keep what will comfortably fit in the space you've designated to store your containers. My storage container drawer is one that easily can fill up and become difficult to navigate, which is why I suggest biannual purging and reorganizing.

Special Zones

Once I started dividing my kitchen into sections based on function, my cooking routine just felt so much calmer and more streamlined. Think about what you cook and do in the kitchen most often, then make sure your tools and/or ingredients are categorized and separated into spaces to suit these most frequent needs. Beyond obvious zones like the fridge and pantry, there are other more niche zones that could make an impact on your daily routine. The groupings that follow are where I find myself creating in the kitchen most often, but this is personal so consider what other zones can make your time in the kitchen more enjoyable.

goods, and while I empathize that getting rid of items you have had for a long time can be a painful process, once you invest in a good set of airtight, stackable glass containers, you'll never look back. They're easy to store, and food can be safely stored and reheated in them.

Opening the fridge or freezer to discover a stack of these beauties filled with your prepped food or leftovers looks organized and dare I say beautiful. It's a downright soothing experience. They also last—and look good!—forever.

There are many glass container companies out there with varying price points. Wean Green (with their tempered glass and assortment of brightly colored lids), Pyrex, and OXO are a few of the brands I trust most. A variety of sizes is key, so that you are prepared for the times when you make a huge pot of stew that you want to refrigerate or freeze for a meal later in the week, or for when you have a tiny extra bit of salad dressing, and everything in between.

COFFEE, TEA, SPARKLING WATER STATION

Making coffee and tea can be a pleasurable daily ritual. Most days, just the idea of coffee makes me pop out of bed and bolt to the kitchen. Our mornings are choreographed to the second in order to get everyone's tush out the door, so having my press, beans, grinder, sweeteners/syrups, and mugs grouped together is a lifesaver from a time and sanity perspective. I take my (decaf) coffee very seriously, yet by two P.M., I'm on my way to cup after cup of tea. Whether a friend is coming over, or the kids want a cup, having a drawer full of various teas is a nice and visually calming benefit.

We also go through a lot of sparkling water. While it's easy to grab cans of flavored or plain sparkling water, using a sparkling water maker saves a good deal of money over time and the bottles look orderly in your fridge. If desired, use a squeeze of fresh citrus to naturally flavor the water.

SMOOTHIE STATION

If you read my book *Smoothie Project*, you know just how passionate I am about smoothies at any time of day. When I first started making them, I found myself traversing the kitchen gathering ingredients (the pantry for nuts, an overhead cabinet for collagen and protein powder, the freezer for frozen fruits and veg). By dedicating an entire shelf right next to our fridge and freezer to my smoothie stash, I went from a prep and blend time of ten minutes down to five, just by getting organized and intentionally grouping items based on their most common use.

BACK STORAGE: CANNED AND BOTTLED BEVERAGES

Be it soft drinks, kombucha, bottled iced tea, beer, or, hopefully, a good bottle of wine to enjoy after you've reorganized your kitchen, we all have our drink preferences. Depending on the size of your space,

there are a plethora of strategies for housing drinks. I keep most of ours in the back pantry and restock the fridge with just what we will need for two or three days max. I put bottles of wine upright on the top shelf of our fridge, as it's the tallest shelf space, or on the bottom, on their sides. A clear, refillable storage box that holds a dozen cans of soft drinks sits on another shelf. Alternatively, if you have space in your kitchen or close to the place you entertain most often, a small drink refrigerator is a handy luxury for keeping drinks.

ACTIVITY CENTER

When you have kids, especially young ones, it's wise to keep plenty of activities nearby for them to entertain themselves with while you're cooking. I have cubbies in our kitchen outfitted with bins that my kids can pull out, stocked with art supplies, crayons, pens, colored pencils, wood blocks, small toys, balls, and musical instruments.

KIDS' STUFF

I used to be a hot mess when it came to the volume of plates, lunch boxes, water bottles, and other food related kid gear layered in with the adult dishware all over my kitchen. Just putting everything away when unloading the dishwasher was a project. Now I have relegated these items to a large, deep, bin-divided lower shelf so I can easily find what I need (or even send the kids to fetch these items themselves). It's added years to my life.

BAKING STATION

I bake at least once a week, enjoying a bit now and, of course, freezing some for a rainy day. Generally, it's seasonal muffins, breakfast cookies, brownies, or a Bundt cake, but I'm an equal opportunist when it comes to any sort of baked good. I devoted a pull-out drawer in my kitchen to all of my baking

ingredients, like chocolate chips, chunks, and disks; flavor extracts; baking soda and powder; salts, molasses, and much more. I keep most of them in labeled glass jars so I can easily see everything. Being able to see everything gets me jazzed to bake, and even get creative.

In a large, adjacent drawer, I store all of my baking cookware and accessories.

BANQUET/SEATING NOOK

When I was little, a few of my friends had kitchen nooks where they ate as a family. I loved how cozy and comfortable they were and dreamed of having one. When I moved into my own home, it was one of the first things I created. Underneath the kitchen bench are deep drawers where I store board games and puzzles, so we can pull them out to play at the table. But don't stop there; the extra space can hold additional kitchen gear.

NURSING STATION

Whether you breast or bottle feed your baby, a nursing station setup in the kitchen for prepping and cleaning bottles and pumping equipment saves time and avoids some of the stress that come with having a new baby at home. Set up a drying rack specially made for bottles, if possible, next to the sink. Nearby, keep a bottle-cleaning sponge brush, gentle cleaning dish soap, bottles, nipples, and, if nursing, milk storage bags. I also recommend keeping a favorite mug and a container of nursing or chamomile tea nearby too.

KITCHEN SHRINE

I realize this may sound unusual, but over the years I've discovered that if I have something that I love in front of me while I cook, I'm immediately more relaxed. This can be a vase of seasonal flowers, a

candle to light as you begin cooking, a photo of someone you love, a speaker playing your go-to playlist, a box of favorite salts, or even a tiny Buddha. I mix it up depending on my mood to keep feeling engaged and inspired.

JUNK DRAWER

There is no point denying it. We all have a kitchen junk drawer. There is no shame in it and having a catch-all space for items that don't quite fit in the above zones is useful—until you can barely get the drawer open, that is. Then it's time to rethink what lives in there. My essentials? Sticky notes, keys, pens, rubber bands, and hair ties to keep my hair up while I cook. It will look different to everyone, but if you can keep it to a minimum, it won't be a production every time you need to write a note.

For Small Spaces and Beyond

This section is devoted to smaller kitchens, where one is forever trying to maximize every square inch of space (ceilings, backs of doors, even above the oven range). These strategies can help, no matter the size of your space. Here are some ideas for how to make your space work for you.

Open shelving: Open wall shelving can be prone to visual clutter, but I believe it actually can help you avoid crowding. Knowing you can't hide mess behind a cabinet door disciplines you to really consider what you need. Especially in a galley or small kitchen space, open shelving is also a great way to have the essentials right at your fingertips and give your kitchen a clean, open look and feel.

Knife magnet: You don't have to be a gourmet chef to hang knife magnet strips on your wall. Not only do they look sleek and come in different lengths, they're also incredibly utilitarian. Make sure not to overcrowd it, though. Pick a few go-to knives and let them be the stars of the show.

Hanging racks: No matter what size your kitchen, pot and pan racks are a strategic way to organize your cookware. They make it easy to grab a pan as you need it and eliminate the need to stuff cabinets and drawers with oversized, unwieldy pots and pans.

Pegboards: For years I lived in New York City, the small kitchen capital of the world. It was there where I first saw tiny kitchen spaces maximized through the use of pegboards. Available in almost any size, pegboards allow you to dedicate an entire wall space to storage, and with the help of fun-looking hooks, hang everything from pots and pans to bins, to hold your keys, to wire baskets for accessories, coffee mugs, whisks, and more. You can create an efficient kitchen space inexpensively using this approach. If you're in need of ideas, search Pinterest for "pegboard kitchen inspiration." There's lots of awesome examples to help get you started.

Pegboards can be made from different types of materials such a metal, polypropylene, and wood. Wood is an affordable option that's easy to paint in fun colors if you're looking to give a wall an extra something, or to paint it in the same shade as your wall. After all, Julia Child's blue, copper cookware-covered pegboard endures. Need I say more?

Door racks: These racks hang over the top of kitchen or pantry doors, essentially creating a new wall of storage perfect for paper towels, cooking utensils, and more. Affordable, they keep essentials within reach.

A System That Works for Everyone

After you've organized all your spaces, if you want this to last in the long term, you need to ensure your work takes into account the preferences of your family members, explain how the systems work, and get their buy-in to help maintain them. This is particularly critical for your fridge. I am diligent about stocking my fridge once a week, usually on Sundays. However, between having a big eating family of five, all with crazy schedules, and running two food businesses partially out of my home kitchen, our fridge is heavily trafficked. Before I had implemented a good organizational system, that high usage resulted in the fridge interior appearing progressively more chaotic and depressing as the week progressed.

I eventually realized that every time I stocked the fridge/freezer/pantry, I was creating an order that worked *for me*. It failed to take into consideration the four other humans with whom I live. If I buried my husband's favorite yogurt at the back of the fridge, forcing him to excavate past my baskets of figs, little gem lettuce heads, and pickled okra to find it, why was I ever surprised at week's end that nothing was where it started? I was as guilty in this problem as everyone else in my family.

It took time to develop an organizational strategy that accounted for everyone, but once I did, I immediately saw a marked improvement in how orderly the fridge stayed. One key was realizing

that even though I stored all of our leftovers in see-through glass food containers, you still had to remove them to really see what each one contained. Similarly, although I was diligent about keeping all of the sauces, dressings, and condiments, consigned to the door shelves, nobody was aware that I had a system in place, so why should they remember to return the hot sauce to the condiments section? Once I got a bit of input from my family, I created new zones and *labeled them* clearly by category. After that, finding items in the fridge was easier for everyone.

It's not a fail-proof system, especially when kids are factored into the equation. You need to breathe through those occasions when you finally find the Dijon mustard is with the nut butters. Patience is required, as is setting a time once a week—preferably when you restock after visiting the market—to do a bit of maintenance. That day for me is Sunday, when, after a full haul at the farmers market, I make it my mission to pull out whatever food remains on the shelves, wipe it down, and restock adhering to the zone system. Then I am free to meal plan my heart out.

Keep It Fresh: Food Storage

You can buy the highest quality, freshest food on the planet, but if you don't know how to store it properly, you're wasting money and time, not to mention valuable nutrients.

Storing your food to maximize freshness requires different strategies depending on where (e.g., fridge, freezer, pantry) and what you are storing (e.g., berries have different storage than greens do).

FRUITS AND VEGETABLES

First, only washing fruits and vegetables right before you're ready to eat them helps extend their shelf life (if you're going to be consuming them within two days of purchase, it's OK to wash and store).

Second, depending on the type of produce, there are specific ways to store each that will maximize their freshness. Below are the produce I use most frequently and how I keep them fresh as long as possible. If you store produce using these methods, you can extend the shelf life of most by up to two or more weeks, removing excess moisture to keep them crisp, fresh, and bright. Again, be mindful of what your family consumes the most and let that dictate where you put it. For example, we go through a lot of avocados, apples, and salad greens, so I make those easily accessible to everyone. Less frequently used produce goes in the crisper or labeled storage containers. Also, you can make use of the plastic bags your produce comes in from the grocery, or you can invest in reusable cotton or mesh cloth bags.

Apples: Apples will stay fresh for two months or more when refrigerated.

Avocados: Keep avocados on the counter until they have a slight give when you (gently) squeeze

be washed before or after rolling. Hearty greens like kale, Swiss chard, and collard and mustard greens will last longer than more delicate lettuces and greens (like Bibb or spring mix); however, hearty greens can be quite bulky when rolled, so you can also chop and sauté some or all when you purchase them and refrigerate in airtight containers to use in other dishes like Kitchen Sink Pasta (page 176) or Any Veggie Frittata (page 60).

Fresh herbs: Treat herbs like cilantro, dill, parsley, and basil as if they were flowers: Trim the bottoms and place them in a tall glass, with a few inches of water, on the counter. If you change the water once or twice, they can last two weeks or more. If you live in a warm climate, store the herbs in the refrigerator in the same way. Want to hold on to your herbs even longer? See my freezing tip on page 44.

Mushrooms: Line a small brown paper bag with a paper towel, place the mushrooms inside, and store in the fridge. Depending on the variety, they can last anywhere from one to two weeks. (E.g., shiitakes will last much longer than, say, cremini and button mushrooms.)

Stone fruit: Keep peaches, apricots, nectarines, and plums on the counter until they give a little when you gently squeeze them. Then transfer them to the refrigerator for up to two weeks.

Note for all: When you're ready to wash your produce, place it in a strainer and rinse. Transfer to a kitchen towel to dry and you're ready to go. Alternatively, you can fill a large bowl of water to rinse vegetables and then place them on a towel to dry.

When in Doubt, Throw It Out!
Whether storing items in the refrigerator or pantry, checking best-by dates is key. I'm so averse to wasting food, that when I've found food in my fridge that's months past its expiration date, I've eaten it. However, on one of those occasions, I got violently ill after eating a bowl of oatmeal with oats I didn't

them. At that point transfer them to the fridge until ready to use. They will remain fresh and green there up to a week longer.

Bananas: Keep them separate from other fruit on the counter as they are sensitive to the ethylene gas treleased by other fruit and vegetables and will thus ripen faster. As soon as brown spots appear, transfer the bananas to the fridge for up to one week (the skin will turn brown in the fridge, but the banana is fine) or break them out, using my tip on page 44, and freeze for up to three months.

Berries: Line the bottom of an airtight container with a folded paper towel (preferably unbleached). Place unwashed berries in the container, cover with a piece of folded paper towel, and then seal the lid, leaving a small opening so that excess moisture can be released, and refrigerate.

Greens and lettuce: Lay out a long sheet of paper towel (preferably unbleached) and top with fresh greens, roll it up and place in a zip-top bag, leaving an opening for air to circulate. Greens can

realize were three years past their sell-by date. While plenty of things can be eaten past the best-by date, I always err on the side of caution. Trust your eyes and nose before eating it. If you're not sure, toss it. The cost of wasted food is always less than a trip to the doctor's office.

Food Storage Hacks

Food storage clips: I can't be the only parent who discovers bags of pretzels and chips left open, stale, and stuffed into some corner of the pantry. Food storage clips are a lifesaver for everything from securing parchment paper to glass baking dishes to rolling up a half-eaten bag of chips.

Beeswax reusable eco friendly food wraps: Enough with the endless amounts of plastic wrap you go through each year and try these reusable food wraps. They wrap everything from half an avocado to bowls of soups and stews.

Painters' tape and a Sharpie: Mystery leftovers in your fridge? Just slap on a strip of painters' tape and use a Sharpie to label it with a title and a date. When it's finished and you're ready to wash the container, just peel off the tape—no sticky residue to worry about.

Silicone bags: This reusable plastic alternative comes in a wide range of shapes and sizes and is light and flexible, which can be a real plus when you are taking some food to go for the day and don't want to lug around a heavy glass container. I store everything in them, from lettuce to sauces and soups (yes, liquids), snacks for on-the-go, even smoothie ingredients, and they're easy to label. Clean them in the dishwasher or hand wash and dry with a towel. The best part is they eliminate waste and help the environment.

Freezer Specific Storage and Tips

It's not just a home for four-year-old bags of frozen peas (which I know you already discarded in Stage 1!) and ice cream: Your freezer is actually the most magical tool in your meal prep magic arsenal. Most recipes in this book can be frozen for months and defrosted when you need a satisfying meal in minutes. Additionally, having a constant supply of frozen fruits, vegetables, and meats saves time and money when you're prepping meals for the week and gives you the ability to control portion size with no waste. When my kids were younger and I was introducing their palettes to a variety of fruits and vegetables, I would take out just a small handful of frozen broccoli to defrost instead of using a whole bag. Most frozen produce is harvested and flash frozen at its peak, so contrary to what you might believe, it's often fresher and more nutrient dense than what you will find in the produce aisle.

Here's a brief road map for how to conform your freezer to your new meal prep system:

ESSENTIAL GEAR

+ Sharpie and a roll of painters' tape (for labeling)

+ Mason jars in a variety of sizes (great for storing soups and stews in large or individual-size servings)

+ Plastic shoe bins (for organizing your frozen fruit and veggies and being able to easily find what you need)

+ Zip-top bags

+ Glass containers with airtight lids

+ Ice cube trays or individual tempered glass cubes with airtight lids (ideal for freezing fresh baby food, fresh herbs, juice, coffee, or tea cubes, etc.)

+ Popsicle molds (In addition to pops, I freeze leftover/unfinished smoothies to have later for a healthy dessert.)

+ Quarter-size baking sheets (for freezing cut up fruit and veggies so they don't stick together before transferring to zip-top bags)

+ Unbleached parchment paper (prevents frozen produce from sticking to your baking sheet and makes for easy cleanup)

FROZEN MEATS AND SEAFOOD

I keep bags of pre-frozen large, peeled, and deveined shrimp; salmon filets; ground or breasts of chicken and turkey; and steaks in my freezer at all times. Defrosting time varies depending on size, but the general rule of thumb is to transfer them to the refrigerator overnight to defrost—or, if you're in a hurry, submerging them (in their packaging, except for shrimp, which can be placed directly in the water) in a bowl filled with room temperature water. Allow

the meat to defrost until it feels soft and pliable. If you need the food even faster than that, change the water two to three times until it is fully defrosted. And if you're in a real pinch for time (like you needed that meal ready five minutes ago), remove the food from its packaging, place it on a plate, and defrost using the appropriate settings on your microwave (check your appliance's instructions, or on the manufacturer's website, as microwaves tend to operate differently). When using this method, keep an eye on the food to make sure it doesn't start cooking.

FROZEN FRUITS

If you read *Smoothie Project* or follow Weelicious on social media, you know that my family cycles through so much frozen fruit that I basically buy it in bulk. I organize it by type and store it in labeled, translucent plastic shoe boxes, which makes finding what you need a snap, and lets you see what you're out of when making your grocery list. We use frozen fruits to make smoothies, nice creams, and fruit purees to defrost and add to yogurt, and to make a variety of recipes like Mango Morning Glory Muffins (page 143), Smoothie Ice Pops (page 144), and my son's favorite dessert, Any Fruit Crisp (page 147), which he also begs me to let him eat for breakfast.

FROZEN VEGETABLES

You can whip up super quick, delicious meals using the frozen vegetables in your freezer. Lentil Pot Pie (page 140), Cauliflower Fried Rice (page 136), and Crispy Artichoke Hearts with Caesar Dip (page 139) are just a few of my frequent go-tos. As I mentioned above, on nights when I want to ensure that I get a serving of vegetables on my kids' plates, I simply defrost just what I need in the microwave (or put them in a bowl, cover with boiling water, and let them reach my desired doneness), and top them with my favorite seasoning(s) to give whatever I'm serving a hit of extra flavor.

HOT (I MEAN, COLD) TIP

Find yourself at the end of the week with surplus fresh, overly ripe, or spotty fruits or vegetables? Freeze them! Simply chop the fruit into small pieces, arrange them on parchment-lined baking sheets, and freeze overnight. (For vegetables, lightly steam before freezing.) Then, transfer to zip-top bags labeled with the contents and freezing date and keep for up to four months. Frozen bananas can be used in everything from smoothies to nice creams to dipping in melted chocolate (!). I find it faster to run your finger straight down the middle, starting at the tip, which separates the bananas into spears, which you can then break up into smaller pieces that freeze easily.

MORE FREEZING TIPS

✦ Whenever you are making cookie dough, make some extra or save half, roll it into a log, wrap in parchment paper, and freeze for later. Whenever you want a few cookies—or just one—slice what you need and bake as directed, adding an extra minute to the baking time.

✦ When making pesto, baby food, coffee, or leftover sauces, freeze them in ice cube trays or individual tempered glass cubes. If you're leaving for vacation or have milk that's close to its expiration date, you can freeze it this way as well.

✦ When freezing foods, use a Sharpie to label the bag or container with the date to ensure you don't consume it past four months.

✦ Keep a loaf of sliced bread in the freezer. You'll be grateful any time you realize you're out of fresh.

✦ Soups and stews are easy to freeze. Fill individual mason jars three-quarters full of fully cooled soup. To defrost when ready to eat, either place in the refrigerator overnight or in the microwave, heating through to your desired temperature.

✦ Whenever I make Chocolate Raspberry Sheet-Pan Pancake (page 68) or Easy Overnight Belgian Waffles (page 76), I cut them into individual squares and then freeze, so I can just pop them into the toaster as needed. They also make for great sandwich "bread" as a lunchbox addition.

✦ When buying grains, store them in the freezer for at least ten days to kill off any larvae that may have found a home at the grocery store (gross, I know, but virtually every brand has this). Grains will stay fresh in the freezer in their original packaging or in glass jars for well over a year.

✦ When peeling and chopping vegetables, save the scraps in a designated zip-top bag in the freezer and add to it over time. When the bag is full, place the scraps in a large pot of water, bring to a boil, add a bay leaf, salt, and pepper to taste, and simmer, covered, for about one hour to create homemade vegetable stock for use in soups and stews.

✦ When making Compound Butter (page 135), use what you need, roll the remainder in parchment paper, and freeze in labeled zip-top bags. Use a sharp knife to cut off chunks as needed.

The Food in My Kitchen

Below, sorted by zone and food, is an overview of what I normally keep in my kitchen. It is not meant to be exhaustive, but rather to serve as a source of inspiration if you need one or simply as a guide to refer to if you want to get a sense of how I partition the contents of my zones. However, if you want an exhaustive list, I've created a comprehensive guide on Weelicious that probably lists everything I've ever had in my kitchen!

Go to weelicious.com/mpmextras

REFRIGERATOR

Dairy and Eggs

- Unsalted butter
- Cheeses
- Eggs
- Milks
- Yogurt

Fresh Fruits and Vegetables

Check out the link above to see my full list of fruits and vegetables I keep in the fridge versus the ones I never put in there!

Condiments, Sauces, Dressings, Nut Butters, and Jams

Once opened, I store most jarred and bottled condiments—sauces, nut butters, preserves, etc—on the shelves of my fridge door. I have a complete list of everything on Weelicious at the link above.

PANTRY

- **Vegetables that are best stored in a cool, dry place:** garlic, onions, potatoes, squash
- **Cereals, oats, grains, and dry breakfast items**
- **Breads and baked goods**
- **Rice and grains**
- **Dried beans and pulses**
- **Pasta**
- **Snacks:** popcorn, cookies, pretzels, crackers, dried fruits, etc. Check out the link at left to see the mother of all snack lists!
- **Bottles and jarred condiments:** vinegars; organic olive, vegetable, or canola oil; cooking spray; salts; and unopened sauces, mustards, olives, etc. See link at left for a complete list.
- **Baking ingredients:** flours, sugars, baking soda, baking powder, chocolate, vanilla extract, etc.
- **Canned foods:** anchovies, artichoke hearts, coconut milk, hearts of palm, whole tomatoes, tomato paste, sun-dried tomatoes, canned beans, green chiles, pumpkin puree, roasted red peppers, tuna (water and oil packed), soups, boxed ramen, and broths. These basic, real-food ingredients are some of the most important things to have in your pantry. They are handy for whipping up a quick soup (Ribollita Soup, page 223), burgers (California Black Bean Burgers, page 167), or even brownies (Black Bean Brownie Cookies, page 175).
- **Drinks:** coffee, teas, bottled and canned beverages

FREEZER

- **Dough:** cookie, phyllo, pie crust, pizza, and puff pastry

- **Fruit**

- **Meat**

- **Nuts**

- **Seeds**

- **Seafood**

- **Poultry**

- **Vegetables**

- **Ice cream**

COUNTERTOP

- **Go-to spices, vinegars, and oils:** Don't hide items that you cook with daily, such as salt, pepper, olive oil, etc. I have a lazy Susan right by the oven, on which I keep those items, as well as honey and some small bottles of various cooking oils. I fill up a small bowl with kosher salt to keep on the lazy Susan, while the big box stays in the pantry. You don't have to get a high-quality lazy Susan, but I find it helps make this jumble of bottles and jars aesthetically pleasing.

- **Fruits to ripen,** including bananas, avocados, and stone fruit, or ones that you want to remember to eat as soon as possible, like pineapples and melons. I like to showcase fruit in a pretty bowl.

- **Tomatoes** (beefsteak, heirloom, and/or cherry), both to ripen and avoid the mealy texture a fridge can impart.

SPICE DRAWER

I love my spice drawer. Even when I'm only looking for a specific spice, seeing all of them inspires me to think about how else I can boost the flavor of the dish I'm cooking. Spices should be stored in a cool, dry spot, so they retain their potency. When you cook the recipes in this book, you can view the spice measurements as an approximate guide and let your palate and inventiveness lead the way. Here's what's in my spice drawer week to week, but I encourage you to fill yours with whatever turns you on.

Bay leaves	Garlic powder	Paprika: Hungarian and smoked
Cayenne	Ginger	
Chili powder	Italian mix	Peppercorns
Cinnamon	Onion powder	Pumpkin pie spice
Cumin	Oregano	
Chives	Nutmeg: ground or whole	Rosemary
Crushed red pepper		Thyme
Curry powder		Toasted sesame seeds
Dill		Turmeric

NOTE: *Make sure to use your spices within their lifespan as they lose strength over time. As a rule of thumb, herbs last a year from their sell-by date, ground spices two to three years, and whole spices about four years. The good news? Salt lasts indefinitely!*

STAGE

3 Prep

CONGRATULATIONS. You've just crossed into the culinary equivalent of the Earth's stratosphere. The Purge and Prep stages of your rocket have fallen away, and if you were to look back toward the launch pad (the place where you started this whole meal prep journey), you wouldn't even see it. That's just how far you have come. Take it in and savor that sense of accomplishment. Space lies within your grasp.

Before you begin the prep process, map out your days and make sure you have a clear sense of your upcoming week and what meals you'll be eating at home; lunches, if any, that you'll need to make; and any recipes that can be eaten or repurposed over a several-day period. Make a detailed grocery list based on what you plan on cooking (see an example of one month of meal prep on page 228), making sure to look through your fridge, freezer, and pantry to see what you already have and to ensure you are only buying what you need. If you have implemented the organizational principles from the first two sections of this book, this part will be a breeze, and a kind of fun one at that.

Adding Pep to Your Prep: Strategies for Meal Prep Success

I sit down once a month, usually on a Sunday, to create a calendar of meals, based on variety, ease, and what my family enjoys. We rarely go out to eat during the week, so I need a plan for almost every meal. Planning out a month's worth of meals takes some time but it saves more in the long run. It can be done week to week, but I find it less daunting to do twelve times a year than fifty-two. Start with a paper or online calendar to keep track of what you want to make, accounting for what's already in your freezer, so you put any prepared meals, soups, vegetables, and meats to work, and then consider how you want to supplement the frozen food at your fingertips with fresh ingredients.

At the start of each week, which for me is Sunday, I always:

+ Set aside a few hours to shop, prep ingredients, and review the recipes for the upcoming week, ensuring that I avoid stress and save hours of time in the hectic days to come.

+ Clean out the fridge, removing any leftovers from the prior week(s) to either have for lunch that day or discard. Wipe down fridge shelves and take stock of what I've already got on hand in the fridge, freezer, and pantry.

+ Shop our local farmers' market, where I get more than 80 percent of the food we will eat that week—produce, eggs, cheese, meats, nuts, dried fruits, and more. Often, my kids come with me, pointing out what they're excited to eat, which takes some of the guesswork out of what to buy for them, especially when it comes to snacks. Shopping at a farmers' market is also a great way to make sure you are consuming more fresh food than packaged. Afterwards, I stop by our local grocery to grab whatever extra items are needed.

Once home from the market, here's how I prep for the coming week:

+ Put away produce (see page 39 for specific tips on maximizing freshness during storage).

+ Peel and/or chop the vegetables I plan to cook that week or that my family enjoys snacking on, such as carrots or celery.

+ Roast a sheet pan of vegetables, such as cauliflower, butternut squash, broccoli, or Brussels sprouts.

+ Steam a big batch of rice, pasta, lentils, quinoa, or other grain.

+ Air fry chicken breasts for use in my upcoming recipes or cook chicken in my preferred way (such as Lime Pulled Chicken, page 79, or roasted chicken, page 92).

+ Make chicken stock, possibly using the bones or other leftovers from the chicken prepared above, which could come in handy for meals in the next few days or can be frozen for a later use.

The goal is to prep the components of the dishes you are serving that week. Having ready-to-use ingredients to mix and match into your meals, and only needing to add your favorite sauce or dressing will completely transform your relationship to mealtime.

Digital Kitchen Organization

Cooking can and should be a shared responsibility whenever possible. Using digital tools that are shared between family members helps everyone to be involved and organized.

1. Keep a running list on your phone of your weekly go-to foods, using a shared Google Doc, Doodle Doc, or Notes so other family members can view

it and make requests, and so you always know what you're running low on.

2. Organize your list by category (condiments, produce, grains, canned goods, etc.) for quick reference to make shopping at the grocery even easier.

3. Create a shared online calendar detailing your meals. Family members can add their preferred meals to different nights, and you can assign which family member is responsible for cooking each meal. I like keeping it fun by noting themes, like pasta night and taco Tuesday.

4. Keep a list or spreadsheet of how much you spend on groceries week to week so you can assess and see where you can cut corners to save.

Meal-Specific Prep Tips

BREAKFAST

I generally have 15 to 20 minutes in the morning to get my kids dressed and out the door, so breakfast dishes that can be ready in minutes are my thing. I tend to lean on ready-to-eat breakfasts that can be made ahead like Creamy Chia Pudding (page 71) and Overnight Flight (of Oats), Five Ways (page 196), which can be kept in mason jars in the fridge to enjoy at home or on-the-go. Smoothies made from nutrient-dense ingredients can be whipped up in minutes (faster even with the help of frozen smoothie packs; check out the Double-Chocolate Protein Smoothie recipe, page 72 for tips) and often taste like dessert. Most baked goods like muffins, pancakes, and scones can be frozen for up to three months, so they can be made ahead and reheated in a preheated 250°F (120°C) oven for 15 minutes, or even more quickly in your air fryer or microwave for 1 to 2 minutes. I'm a big fan of Chocolate Granola Breakfast Cookies (page 204) because then we can have cookies for breakfast, which always scores me points. Want an even simpler breakfast? Greek yogurt and granola parfaits or containers of fresh fruit are refreshing and a fast and healthy way to start the day.

LUNCH

Lunch is often the most important and forgotten meal of the day. For my kids' school lunches, I prepare them the night before in bento-style lunch containers. A fruit, vegetable, protein, and carbohydrate should go in every lunch so you're offering a balanced meal, and are making sure the lunch appeals to all the senses, not just taste. A variety of colors and textures engages and interests kids.

Turning Meals at Home into Your Child's Packed Lunch: Often when making breakfast, lunch, or dinner, I will set aside a portion or two of whatever I'm making for my kids' lunches the next day. This might entail simply packing up the leftovers, or I might transform elements from the meal into something new and fun, which ideally doesn't need to be reheated. For instance, I love to transform leftover roast chicken (page 92) into a chicken avocado wrap, toss leftover cooked pasta with pesto, or use leftover rice to make Cheesy Brown Rice Cakes (page 184). I also love to make use of breakfast leftovers by defrosting the extra waffles, pancakes, and French toasts that I've frozen to use as sandwich bread. Lunch can, but of course doesn't always need to, be a sandwich and piece of fruit. A packed lunch that includes a Savory Hand Pie (page 214), Mango Morning Glory Muffins (page 143), or a Breakfast Burrito (page 66) can brighten anyone's day.

Off to Work: If you're trying to save money and/or eat healthier, bringing lunch to work is ideal. You need not make a completely separate dish— rather, consider that the week's other meals can be adapted. You can adhere to the principles above, but know you have less constraints, especially as workplaces often make it easy to warm your food.

In the warmer months, I gravitate toward fresh and light salads. When it's cooler, I lean toward warmer, heartier dishes, usually leftovers from dinners that week, such as vegetarian Stuffed Peppers (page 192), Sheet-Pan Tofu (pages 108–115), or Turkey and Quinoa Chili (page 103)—all of which I find even tastier the next day.

Salad Jars: At all times I've got jars in my fridge filled with everything from chia pudding and overnight oats to, yes, salad. Salad jars are a lunch lifesaver and the options are limitless. Start by placing some dressing at the bottom of a jar and topping it with a heartier ingredient that won't get soggy, like grains or chopped vegetables. Then add greens, nuts, seeds, dried fruits, or cheese—anything you love in your salad. I make a big assembly line of ingredients and jars to make a bunch at once so I can grab and go when needed. On a busy day, when I need something nutritious, I just shake the jar to distribute the dressing all over, open, and devour.

DINNER

The repurpose strategy is key to making dinner simple. For instance, I'll steam a big pot of rice, so I can make Cheesy Brown Rice Cakes (page 184), Leftover Rice Pudding (page 187), or as use a base for Butternut Squash and Chickpea Coconut Curry (page 171). These dishes all make delicious leftovers as well.

Leftovers are a huge part of how I feed my family. I often prefer leftovers to the original, as flavors tend to meld more with a bit of time. Whenever I'm making a recipe, if possible, I increase or even double the ingredients so that I have leftovers for the next couple of days. Sometimes I simply pack up the leftovers to reheat for lunch. Other times I remold what I have made into a new dish. For example, I love to make at least two roast chickens (page 92), one to enjoy that night and one to use for meat for burritos or on top of salad later in the week.

The recipes in the Execute chapter are full of tips that suggest when to make more of a dish, offer ideas for how to repurpose leftovers, and recommend the best ways to reheat. But once you start thinking about cooking in this way, it'll become second nature, and you'll come up with your own best practices.

DESSERTS

Dessert makes everything better, especially when it's healthy. Smoothie Ice Pops (page 144), Any Fruit Crisp (page 147), and Creamy Chia Pudding (page 71) are staples of our weekly dessert rotation that make everyone happy.

Execute

YOU'VE PURGED, organized, and prepped, which means that now you're ready for the fun part. And if "fun" isn't a word you associate with cooking, I hope that you will now, at the very least, come to find this stage considerably easier and far more satisfying than whatever you were doing before finding this book. Either way, if you're now arriving at the Execute section having worked through the first three sections, take a moment to think about and appreciate everything you have accomplished. Even if you don't make your meal plans based on the recipes that follow (I'm obviously *not* recommending that you do that!), and only maintain your newly organized kitchen, you are going to find cooking, and using your kitchen in general, to be a simpler and much more gratifying experience. A user-friendly kitchen is just that—a place that's easier for you and your family to navigate, and in which spending time provides feelings of calm and pleasure.

That being said, I strongly encourage you to explore the entirety of this section and make it work for your particular mealtime needs. Once you start applying the planning and prepping techniques to these recipes, you will see how fully you can reap the fruits of all your hard work.

Many cookbooks are organized by breakfast, lunch, and dinner, but that doesn't always support your needs when you have a surplus of one type of food and you need immediate ideas for what to do with it. When I'm working on meal plans for the week, I tend to try to use what I have on hand and come

up with menus based on those foods. I've divided the recipe section into categories based on the foods that our family uses the most (proteins like chicken and beef, eggs, tofu, fresh vegetables, etc.) and where they are stored (refrigerator, freezer, or pantry), see page 232. This way you can look around your kitchen and utilize the book based on what you have from these categories in your newly organized kitchen, and then focus on a handful of different recipes. If you need some ideas on how it could all fit together, see page 228 for a menu showing a whole month of meal prep.

Recipe Tips and Tricks

The recipes that follow are some of my absolute favorites and are perfectly suited for meal prep. They also are written in a way that includes more advice than you typically find in cookbooks. My goal is to help you get the most of out of these dishes and prepare them in a way that is simple, efficient, and convenient for your schedule. In the recipe tips labeled "To Enjoy Later," you'll find specific instructions on how to store the dish in the fridge and/or freezer and also how to reheat it. "Prep in Advance" offers guidance for how to make certain components of the recipe now, to cut down on cooking time later. And "Repurpose Leftovers" offers ideas for how you can turn a recipe into a completely new dish in the future.

The Big Benefit of Small Kitchen Appliances

As I have mentioned, I love the convenience of appliances like air fryers, which heat up to 400°F (205°C) in seconds and cook in about half the time as a conventional oven; slow cookers, which you can turn on in the morning and walk away from until you're ready to eat dinner with your family; and electric pressure cookers, which offer flavorful braised dishes in no time at all. I use these three appliances regularly in the recipes that follow. But don't worry if the instructions mention an appliance you don't have. I offer plenty of alternative methods, so anyone can make the dish, but I also mention if I think one method generates superior results, so you can adjust your plans accordingly.

More on Mise en Place

I talked about this earlier with respect to organizing your kitchen, and the principles apply here more than anywhere. One of the best strategies I ever learned is to place everything needed for a recipe onto a sheet pan before starting to cook. If you find yourself lost and flustered while cooking, this strategy is for you. Not only does it allow you to focus on cooking, but it also can speed up the process as you won't be desperately searching for that one ingredient you can't locate before your pot boils over. Luckily your kitchen is already organized pro-style, so getting all of your ingredients and cooking tools together shouldn't take long.

Clean as You Go

As much as I absolutely love cooking, I loathe doing dishes. When I walk into someone's house while they are cooking and see bowls, plates, and empty food containers everywhere, or watch one of my kids finish preparing a meal and leaving behind a sink filled to the brim with dirty pots and pans, I can feel my blood pressure starting to climb. When I cook, I make sure to clean every step of the way, so that by the time I have a meal on the table, there's little to do other than clean our plates and silverware. Not only does it make doing the dishes simple, but I enjoy my meal so much more knowing there's almost nothing left to do—other than asking my husband to finish up cleaning the dishes we used during the meal.

Now, what are you waiting for? Go make magic!

PREP TIME
10 minutes

COOK TIME
18 to 20 minutes

SERVES
4 to 6

Any Veggie Frittata

3 cups (720 ml) chopped vegetables (see the * opposite for ideas)

12 large eggs

¼ tablespoon full-fat dairy (*whole milk, cream, sour cream, Greek yogurt, or crème fraîche*)

1 teaspoon kosher salt

Freshly ground black pepper

1 to 2 tablespoons olive oil, for the pan

½ cup shredded cheese (*mozzarella, Monterey Jack, Colby, and/or crumbled feta cheese*)

Fresh chopped herbs (*basil, dill, parsley, tarragon, or chives*), for serving

On those nights . . . wait, did I say "nights"? . . . I mean, for any meal when I can't think of something delicious that I can make fast, the solution is a frittata. While filling this beauty with vegetables is the way I usually go, don't let that limit you. Toss in any cooked protein, such as chicken, shrimp, smoked salmon, or turkey; it's sure to only add to the perfection of this fluffy, one-pan meal. I like to slide the finished frittata onto a cutting board, slice it into wedges, and serve them alongside a green salad and some big hunks of fresh bread.

✦ Preheat the oven to 425°F (220°C).

✦ If using cooked vegetables in your frittata, heat a large skillet over medium heat and reheat the vegetables for 3 to 5 minutes, or until heated through and tender. Set the cooked vegetables aside on a plate.

✦ While the vegetables are reheating, crack the eggs into a large bowl and whisk until creamy and yellow throughout. Add your dairy of choice, 1 teaspoon salt, and pepper to taste and whisk thoroughly to combine.

✦ In the same large skillet over medium heat, add the olive oil and whirl to coat the bottom of the pan. Add the egg mixture and allow to set for 2 to 3 minutes. Distribute the cheese and desired cooked and/or raw vegetables over the egg mixture and transfer to the preheated oven to cook for 12 to 14 minutes, or until puffy, golden, and cooked through.

I love a frittata with as many vegetables as possible. While the recipe calls for frozen, feel free to load up your frittata with any leftover raw or cooked vegetables you have in the fridge. The more vegetables it has, the puffier and more flavorful the frittata will be. Here's a list of my preferred vegetables in this frittata, but let the seasons dictate what you use: sautéed vegetables, such as sliced mushrooms, spinach, diced bell peppers, diced onions, chopped asparagus, chopped broccoli, or diced zucchini; or raw vegetables, such as halved cherry tomatoes, diced avocado, sun-dried tomatoes, diced tomatoes, or sliced scallions.

TO ENJOY LATER

The frittata can be cooled and refrigerated in an airtight container for up to 3 days. To reheat, place slices in a microwave and cook for 30 seconds, in a saucepan over medium heat for 1 minute on each side, or in an air fryer at 350°F (175°C) for 2 minutes.

PREP IN ADVANCE

The vegetables can be cooked and the egg mixture whisked together up to 24 hours before assembling and cooking the frittata. Store them separately in covered airtight containers in the fridge.

Ricotta Soft-Scrambled Eggs

2 tablespoons unsalted butter

6 large eggs

½ cup (125 g) whole-milk ricotta cheese

¼ cup (25 g) freshly grated Parmesan cheese

½ teaspoon kosher salt

Freshly ground black pepper

Scrambled eggs are a classic breakfast choice for a reason—they can be whipped up in a matter of minutes and are delicious and satisfying. And simply adding a bit of ricotta is a real game changer! These next-level eggs are great on their own, but also come in handy when making breakfast burritos, tacos, or sandwiches (see page 64). The ricotta brings out the richness of the eggs, yielding a super-creamy final product. Plus, the ricotta adds flavor and an extra boost of protein, so it's a win-win in my book! This recipe calls for grated Parmesan cheese, too, but feel free to swap it out for your favorite grated cheese.

✦ Melt the butter in a medium nonstick skillet over medium-low heat.

✦ While the butter melts, add the eggs, ricotta, Parmesan, salt, and pepper to a large bowl. Whisk until well combined and no lumps of ricotta remain.

✦ Pour the egg mixture into the skillet and reduce heat to low. Cook, stirring almost constantly, for 3 to 4 minutes, or until the eggs are set and no liquid remains. Serve immediately.

A nonstick or well-seasoned cast-iron pan works best for this recipe, but if you don't have either of those, spray whatever skillet you want to use with a little nonstick spray before adding the butter. Also, the curd of these eggs will be much smaller than traditional scrambled eggs, which is a truly beautiful thing! Resist the urge to cook these eggs further than directed; the key to creaminess is cooking them just until they set.

PREP TIME
25 minutes

COOK TIME
15 minutes

MAKES
12 sandwiches; serves
4 to 6

Pull-Apart Egg Sandwiches
with CRISPY PROSCIUTTO AND PESTO

1 ounce (28 g) thinly
sliced prosciutto

1 (18-ounce/510 g)
package dinner rolls,
cut in half widthwise

⅓ cup (75 ml) pesto
(store-bought or
homemade, page 132)

1 batch Ricotta Soft-
Scrambled Eggs (page
63)

½ tablespoon unsalted
butter, melted

¼ teaspoon garlic
powder

¼ teaspoon dried basil

¼ teaspoon dried
oregano

Crushed red pepper

Flaky salt

Consider this recipe the LBD (gents, that stands for Little Black Dress) of meals. It is perfect for almost any occasion—from an epic brunch when entertaining, to a low-key, weeknight meal when you need something quick and the fridge is bare. I also like to make a big batch of these and save them for a later date. Once they are assembled, stop before baking them, and follow my tips below!

◆ Preheat the oven to 450°F (230°C) and line a rimmed sheet pan with foil.

◆ Cook the prosciutto in a medium skillet over medium heat until crisp, about 2 minutes per side. Remove from the heat and let it cool, then coarsely chop.

◆ Place the bottom halves of the dinner rolls on the prepared sheet pan and spread an even layer of pesto on top of each. Add the scrambled eggs, dividing them evenly, then sprinkle with the crispy prosciutto. Top with the remaining dinner rolls halves.

◆ In a small bowl, combine the melted butter, garlic powder, basil, oregano, crushed red pepper, and flaky salt. Using a pastry brush, distribute the garlic butter evenly on the tops of the rolls.

◆ Bake for 5 minutes, then cut into individual rolls and serve.

If you have a child resistant to bigger flavors like pesto, there's no shame in replacing the pesto with a slather of ketchup or their favorite savory spread.

PREP IN ADVANCE
The scrambled eggs, crispy prosciutto, pesto, and garlic butter can be made up to 24 hours before assembling and baking the sandwiches. Or once the sandwiches are assembled, instead of baking them, wrap the sandwiches tightly in foil. They will keep for up to 2 days in the refrigerator, or up to one month in the freezer. To reheat, place the refrigerated sandwiches in a preheated 350°F (175°C) oven for 5 to 7 minutes. If cooking from frozen, reheat for about 10 to 15 minutes or until warmed throughout.

Freezer-Stash Breakfast Burritos

3 tablespoons olive oil

1 (16-ounce/455 g) bag frozen shredded hash browns

Kosher salt

6 large eggs

½ cup (120 ml) milk

Freshly ground black pepper

1 (12-ounce/340 g) bag frozen sliced onions and bell peppers, or 4 cups (105 g) fresh slices

2 cups (230 g) grated cheddar or Monterey Jack cheese

6 burrito-size flour tortillas

1 (14½-ounce/410 g) can black beans, drained and rinsed

1 cup (240 ml) prepared salsa

½ cup (20 g) loosely packed fresh cilantro (leaves and stems), chopped (optional)

Nonstick cooking spray

Make a batch of these hearty and filling burritos to stash in the freezer—your future self will thank you. Zero chopping is required. I rely on quality frozen veggies to add flavor and keep things super simple.

+ In a large nonstick skillet with a lid, heat 2 tablespoons of the olive oil over medium-high heat. When the oil is hot, add the hash browns and a pinch of salt, cover, and cook for 6 minutes. Flip the shredded potatoes, cover again, and cook for an additional 6 minutes until the potatoes are tender and golden. Season with salt and set aside.

+ Add the eggs and milk to a large bowl and whisk until combined. Season with salt and black pepper. Add the remaining tablespoon olive oil to the skillet and heat to a shimmer. Add the onions and bell peppers and cook for 5 to 7 minutes, or until the vegetables are softened and beginning to brown. Pour the egg mixture over the onions and bell peppers and cook for 2 to 3 minutes, stirring occasionally or until the eggs are scrambled, light, and fluffy. Stir 1½ cups (170 g) of the cheese into the egg mixture until melted. Season to taste with salt and black pepper, then remove from heat.

+ To assemble, spread out a tortilla on a clean work surface, add ⅓ cup (50 g) hash browns, ⅓ cup (60 g) black beans, ½ cup (8 ml) of the egg mixture, 2 tablespoons salsa, and a sprinkle of cilantro, if using, in a rectangle in the middle of the tortilla leaving a few inches around the edge of the tortilla uncovered. Fold in the two sides of the burrito, then starting from the bottom, roll the burrito into a cylinder, sprinkling a heaping tablespoon of cheese right under the seam of the burrito. (This will help the tortilla to seal.) Repeat with the remaining ingredients to assemble the burritos.

+ Heat a large nonstick skillet sprayed with cooking spray over medium heat. Add 2 burritos, seam side down, to the skillet and cook until golden, about 2 minutes. Flip and cook for 2 minutes more. Repeat with the remaining burritos. The burritos are ready to serve, or save them to enjoy later, using the tips at right.

Seal the burritos with a little melted cheddar cheese so everything stays in the burrito while you're eating it.

TO ENJOY LATER

Let the burritos cool to room temperature. Tightly wrap each one in a piece of foil, then store in a freezer-safe bag for up to 3 months.

TO REHEAT

Oven: Preheat to 400°F (205°C) and bake the frozen, wrapped burrito on a sheet pan for 20 to 25 minutes, or until warmed through. **Air Fryer (my fave way!):** Remove foil and heat at 400°F (205°C) for 10 to 12 minutes. **Microwave:** Remove foil, place on a plate, and use the defrost function for 5 minutes, then cook on high for 1 to 2 minutes, or until warm throughout.

PREP TIME
10 minutes

COOK TIME
20 minutes

SERVES
4 to 6

Chocolate Raspberry Sheet-Pan Pancake

4 tablespoons (½ stick/ 55 g) unsalted butter, melted and cooled, plus 1 tablespoon for greasing the baking sheet

3 large eggs

3 cups (720 ml) buttermilk

1 teaspoon vanilla extract

2 tablespoons honey or maple syrup

2⅔ cups (330 g) all-purpose flour

2 teaspoons baking powder

1 teaspoon baking soda

1 teaspoon kosher salt

1 cup (125 g) fresh raspberries

¾ cup (130 g) semisweet or dark chocolate chips or chopped chocolate

Optional toppings: whipped cream, chocolate sauce, maple syrup, honey, or chopped fresh fruit

This dish is essentially a MASSIVE pancake that is the ideal vehicle for anything from fruits to nuts to chocolate. It's a decadent, tender pancake requiring no standing over the griddle or flipping. Cut into squares and serve with your choice of toppings, though its flavor is so major, it's perfect on its own.

+ Preheat the oven to 500°F (260°C).

+ Grease a 13 by 18-inch (33 by 46 cm) baking sheet with half of the extra tablespoon butter. Place a piece of parchment paper on the baking sheet with enough overage on both ends to easily lift it out of the pan once baked and use the remaining half of the tablespoon of butter to grease the parchment. This will make removing the pancake easier.

+ Whisk together the cooled butter, the eggs, buttermilk, vanilla, and honey in a large bowl.

+ In a medium bowl, whisk together the flour, baking powder, baking soda, and salt.

+ Whisk the flour mixture slowly into the buttermilk mixture until just combined.

+ Pour the batter into the prepared baking sheet and sprinkle with the raspberries and chocolate chips.

+ Place the pancake into the oven and immediately reduce the temperature to 400°F (205°C). Bake for 20 minutes or until the pancake puffs and the top starts to turn golden.

+ Cut into squares using a pizza cutter or kitchen shears. Serve immediately with desired toppings.

I've used raspberries and chocolate here, but feel free to get creative with the add-ins: Blueberries, blackberries, strawberries, chopped nuts, chocolate-coated candies, crumbled cooked bacon... you name it, it will be delicious in this! And the same creativity can be exercised on the topping selections.

TO ENJOY LATER
Let cool after baking and refrigerate in an airtight container for up to 3 days. To freeze, cut into squares after it cools and place in labeled zip-top bags. To rewarm, microwave for 30 seconds, place in a preheated 250°F (120°C) oven for 5 minutes, or heat in an air fryer at 350°F (175°C) for 2 minutes.

PREP IN ADVANCE
The whisked dry ingredients can be stored covered. The combined wet ingredients can be refrigerated overnight.

REPURPOSE LEFTOVERS
Cut the pancake into identical square shapes and use as sandwich "bread." Slather with your nut butter of choice, jelly, cream cheese, etc. for an epic sandwich.

Creamy Chia Pudding, Four Ways

BASE RECIPE INGREDIENTS

2 cups (240 ml) milk of choice

½ cup (80 g) chia seeds

1 teaspoon vanilla extract

¼ cup (60 ml) maple syrup or honey

One thing you will always find in my fridge is chia seed pudding. That may not be what you expected me to say, but my youngest child wants it for breakfast, in her school lunch, and/or as a dessert several days a week. What makes this chia pudding recipe so special? Preparing it in your blender. Unlike normal chia pudding, this one is pureed, which makes it super creamy. You may find the texture similar to the vanilla pudding you had as a kid, only this one is made entirely with wholesome ingredients. Also, chia seeds deliver a nice bit of protein and are fiber packed, meaning (spoiler alert) they'll help to keep you regular too.

FLAVOR IDEAS

1. **Raspberry Chia Pudding:** Add 1 cup (125 g/140 g) fresh or frozen raspberries to the blender.

2. **Chocolate–Peanut Butter Chia Pudding:** Mix in 2 tablespoons cocoa powder plus 2 tablespoons peanut butter.

3. **Vanilla Bean Chia Pudding:** Slice a vanilla bean in half. Using a small knife, scrape the seeds into the blender.

4. **Matcha Chia Pudding:** Add 2 tablespoons matcha powder.

+ Place the base recipe ingredients in a blender, add your flavor option of choice, and puree until smooth.

+ Divide among 4 glasses or jars and refrigerate, covered, for at least 1 hour before serving.

I sometimes like to double the base pudding recipe and add any extra flavors later. I store it in a large airtight container in the fridge and stir in the raspberries and puree with the cocoa powder, vanilla bean, and/or matcha flavors right before serving, so we can have different versions of the pudding each day.

TO ENJOY LATER
The pudding can be refrigerated in an airtight container for up to 5 days before serving.

Double-Chocolate Protein Smoothie

1 medium banana, frozen

½ cup (90 g) frozen cauliflower florets

2 tablespoons unsweetened cacao powder

2 tablespoons cacao nibs, carob, or chocolate chips

1 date, pitted, or 1 tablespoon maple syrup

1 serving collagen peptides

1½ cups (360 ml) milk of choice

If you read my last cookbook, *Smoothie Project*, you know how passionate I am about my daily smoothie. In my opinion, smoothies are the best and easiest way to ensure you are getting maximum nutrition in your diet. Given my obsession with nutritious blender drinks, I'm always creating new flavor combinations. This particular recipe has become one of my girls' most requested smoothies, with two types of unsweetened chocolate (you never can have too much chocolate in my book), protein in the form of collagen peptides for healthy skin and hair, and natural sweetener. If the frozen cauliflower is giving you pause, trust me on this. It makes smoothies even creamier, but its taste is undetectable. Also, believe it or not, cauliflower has 4 grams of protein per cup and very few calories. This one is a total win!

Place the ingredients in a blender and puree until creamy.

To make your smoothie truly irresistible, top it with a handful of granola or your favorite cereal and serve it with a spoon.

TO ENJOY LATER
Smoothies can be made pureed the night before, poured into serving glasses, and covered until ready to drink. Or, after pureeing the smoothies, divide the mixture among ice pop molds (two or more, depending on size) and freeze for 4 hours or overnight.

PREP IN ADVANCE
Make smoothie packs that you can use to prepare smoothies in a snap later. Put the cauliflower florets, cacao powder, cacao nibs, date, and collagen peptides in labeled zip-top bags and freeze for up to 4 months. When ready to enjoy, place the frozen ingredients plus the milk of your choice in a blender and puree.

REPURPOSE LEFTOVERS
Pour smoothie into popsicle molds and freeze overnight.

PREP TIME
10 minutes

COOK TIME
20 minutes

SERVES
4 to 6

Stovetop Broccoli Mac and Cheese

Kosher salt

1 head broccoli, florets only, chopped into bite-size pieces (about 2 cups/140 g)

1 pound (455 g) medium pasta shells

4 tablespoons (½ stick/55 g) unsalted butter

¼ cup (30 g) all-purpose flour

5 cups (1.2 liters) whole milk

8 ounces (225 g) sharp cheddar cheese, grated (about 2 cups)

½ cup (50 g) grated Parmesan cheese

Remember when your mom splurged on the fancy mac and cheese? You know, the kind that came with shell noodles and the creamy package of cheese sauce? That was a BIG day. Now you can recreate the excitement of finding a box of that packaged gold in the pantry with this quick-to-whip-up and better-for-you stovetop mac and cheese recipe. It's hard to make too much of this so consider doubling the recipe for meals later in the week. Bonus points for adding extra veggies!

✦ Bring a large pot of salted water to a boil. Add the broccoli and cook for 2 minutes, or until bright green and tender. Remove from the water with a slotted spoon and drain thoroughly. Set aside.

✦ To the same pot of water, add the pasta and par cook for 5 minutes, until still firm to the bite, then drain and set aside.

✦ Return the pot to the stovetop over low heat and melt the butter. Once melted, stir in the flour and then cook for 2 minutes, or until the mixture is golden in color and begins to smell nutty. Add the milk and a generous pinch of salt and bring to a boil. Add the par-cooked pasta and reduce heat to a simmer. Cook, stirring frequently, for 7 to 10 minutes, or until the pasta is tender and the milk has reduced to create a thick and creamy sauce.

✦ Remove from heat and stir in the reserved broccoli and both cheeses. Stir until the cheeses have melted and everything is well combined.

You can use any vegetable you fancy, fresh or frozen, to replace the broccoli. Simply cook your vegetables of choice (some ideas: peas, cauliflower, zucchini, carrots, or onions), cut into bite-size pieces, and stir them into the finished mac and cheese before serving. I like to blanch delicate vegetables like peas and air fry heartier vegetables like cauliflower. Also, if you want a substantial dose of veg, feel free to double the quantity. Any cooked meats, such as crumbled bacon, shredded rotisserie chicken, or chopped ham or turkey, can be added too.

If you want to add a little extra hit of flavor, stir 1 teaspoon Dijon mustard into the finished dish along with a pinch of cayenne pepper or hot sauce.

TO ENJOY LATER

The mac and cheese can be cooled and then refrigerated in an airtight container for up to 3 days. To rewarm, microwave for 30 to 60 seconds or place in a pot on the stovetop over low to medium heat, stirring occasionally for 3 to 5 minutes, or until warmed through, adding more milk if necessary to loosen the sauce.

Easy Overnight Belgian Waffles

PREP TIME
15 minutes, plus an overnight rise

COOK TIME
30 minutes

MAKES
about 24 waffles (depending on size of your waffle iron)

2½ cups (600 ml) milk, warmed to 100°F (40°C)

4 tablespoons (½ stick/55 g) unsalted butter, melted

3 tablespoons sugar

1 teaspoon active dry yeast

2 large eggs

1 tablespoon vanilla extract

2½ cups (315 g) whole-wheat flour

1 teaspoon ground cinnamon

1 teaspoon kosher salt

FOR SERVING
Pure maple syrup

Whipped cream

Fresh berries

At the start of the COVID lockdown, I panic-purchased a gigantic bag of active dry yeast, and I've been using it little by little ever since. I think of this recipe as a pandemic silver lining. Needing ways to make everyday life at home feel special, these waffles seemed to do just that. The batter is a breeze to assemble; it rises overnight in the fridge so you can start your day to the smells of yeasty, delicious waffles. What's better than that?

✦ Add the milk and butter to a large bowl (that will comfortably fit in your fridge). Sprinkle in the sugar and yeast, then whisk to combine. Let sit for 5 minutes to ensure the yeast is active.

✦ Once the yeast is foamy and activated, add the eggs and vanilla, and whisk until combined. Add the flour, cinnamon, and salt, and whisk to combine. Cover and place in the fridge for at least 8 hours.

✦ When ready to serve, preheat a waffle iron. Once hot, fill with batter and cook the waffle according to the manufacturer's instructions. Remove to a plate. Repeat with remaining batter.

✦ Serve warm with maple syrup, whipped cream, and/or fresh berries.

If the yeast doesn't foam up after 5 minutes (it should be like the head on the top of a draft beer!), it may be dead and unusable. Better to discover that immediately, rather than the next morning when you have a hungry crew waiting for waffles! Also, when I call for a large bowl in the directions for this recipe, I mean it. I learned the lesson of insufficient bowl size the hard way one morning when a batch expanded overnight!

TO ENJOY LATER
Waffles can be cooked, cooled, and then refrigerated in an airtight container for up to 3 days. To freeze, place the waffles in labeled zip-top bags for up to 4 months. To rewarm, microwave the waffles for 30 seconds, place in a preheated 250°F (120°C) oven for 5 minutes, or in an air fryer at 350°F (175°C) for 2 minutes.

PREP IN ADVANCE
You can make the waffle batter up to 24 hours before cooking. Cover and refrigerate.

REPURPOSE LEFTOVERS
Slather waffles with your favorite spread to make epic sandwiches.

PREP TIME
5 minutes

COOK TIME
4 hours

SERVES
4 to 6

Lime Pulled Chicken

4 skinless, boneless chicken breasts

1 (4-ounce/115 g) can green chiles, chopped

1 teaspoon kosher salt

2 cloves garlic, chopped

2 small onions, diced

1 teaspoon ground cumin

Juice of 1 lime

½ cup (20 g) chopped fresh cilantro

Freshly ground black pepper

1 cup (240 ml) chicken broth or Liquid Gold Chicken Stock (page 86)

When I think about easy multipurpose recipes, this pulled chicken is the first one that comes to mind. I simply toss the ingredients into my multi-cooker around midday and by the time I come home later that afternoon, my kitchen not only smells like citrus-herb heaven, but I also have tender, flavorful chicken that I can serve with a leftover grain, salsa, and whatever other toppings I have in my fridge. I really like this chicken in tacos, burritos, or bowls along with rice, beans, guacamole, salsa, grated cheese, sour cream, pickled onions, and more. This delicious chicken is as versatile and kid friendly as it gets.

✦ Place all of the ingredients in a slow cooker. Cover and set the slow cooker to low for 4 hours or high for 2 hours. (*Alternatively, place the ingredients in a large stockpot, bring to a boil, and then reduce heat to a simmer for 20 to 25 minutes, or until the chicken is cooked through. Or alternatively, preheat the oven to 350°F [175°C]. Place the ingredients in a 9 by 11-inch [23 by 28 cm] baking dish. Cover and bake for 30 minutes, or until the chicken is cooked through.*)

✦ When the chicken is cool enough to handle, take two forks and shred the chicken into bite-size pieces. (*Alternatively, use a hand mixer to shred the chicken. It really works! Serve immediately or save for a rainy day.*)

Chicken thighs work great here too. Just add 1 hour to the cooking time.

To get more juice out of your lime, roll it out with the palm of your hand on the counter to release more juice before cutting the lime in half. Bottled lime juice can be substituted for fresh.

TO ENJOY LATER
The chicken can be cooled and then refrigerated in an airtight container for up to 3 days. Place it in the microwave and reheat for 1 minute or in a covered pot for 2 minutes, or until warmed through. Cooked chicken can also be placed in labeled zip-top bags and frozen for up to 4 months. Defrost overnight then add to your favorite recipes.

PREP IN ADVANCE
The ingredients can be placed in a large zip-top bag and refrigerated for up to 2 days or frozen for up to 3 months. Use any of the above cooking methods, adding 5 minutes to the cook time if cooking from frozen on the stovetop or baking.

REPURPOSE LEFTOVERS
Chicken can be placed in taco shells or on crunchy lettuce drizzled with Citrus Cilantro Vinaigrette (page 127) or in a grain bowl.

PREP TIME
10 minutes, plus 4
hours to overnight for
marinating

COOK TIME
15 minutes

SERVES
4

Buttermilk-Brined Chicken Nuggets

with SPECIAL SAUCE

1½ pounds (680 g) skinless, boneless chicken breasts, cut into 1-inch (2.5 cm) pieces

1½ cups (360 ml) buttermilk

1 cup (125 g) all-purpose flour

1 cup (85 g) panko

1 teaspoon garlic powder

1 teaspoon paprika

1¼ teaspoon kosher salt

Freshly ground black pepper

Nonstick cooking spray

1 large pickle, finely chopped, plus 1 tablespoon juice

½ cup (120 ml) sour cream or plain Greek yogurt

1 teaspoon dried dill, or 1 tablespoon fresh dill

This recipe is my answer to boxed frozen chicken nuggets. Do they take a few minutes to prepare? Yes. Are they the best chicken nuggets you'll ever eat? One hundred percent and then some. For starters, if you're not already in the habit of brining your chicken, every nibble of these delectable crunchy bites will convince you that you need to change your ways. The buttermilk helps to tenderize the nuggets so that they can crisp up outside while still retaining moisture. And forget the bottled sauces you're used to serving alongside boxed nuggets. This special magic sauce is going to be your secret weapon, not just for these nuggets but for every food that needs a little dippin' love. You can make these in the oven, if you don't have an air fryer, but air frying is definitely my preferred method.

+ Place the chicken and buttermilk in a large bowl, cover, and refrigerate for 4 hours or overnight.

+ Place the flour, panko, garlic powder, paprika, 1 teaspoon salt, and pepper in a shallow bowl and whisk to combine. Place the chicken nuggets in the panko mixture and toss to completely coat with the dry ingredients.

+ Place the nuggets evenly in the air-fryer basket. Do not overcrowd the nuggets; cook them in batches if necessary. Coat each piece with cooking spray and cook at 375°F (190°C) for 13 to 15 minutes or until golden. *(Alternatively, you can place the nuggets on a parchment or foil-lined baking sheet, coat with cooking spray, and bake in a 400°F [205°C] oven for 18 to 20 minutes or until golden.)*

+ In the meantime, mix together the pickle, sour cream, the remaining ¼ teaspoon salt, and the dill in a bowl. Serve the dipping sauce with the nuggets.

Chicken thighs work great too. Just make sure to cook them for an additional 4 minutes, or until cooked through.

TO ENJOY LATER

Cool the cooked nuggets and refrigerate them in airtight containers for up to 3 days. Reheat in an air fryer at 375°F (190°C) for 2 minutes or in a preheated 300°F (150°C) oven for 3 to 5 minutes or until heated through.

PREP IN ADVANCE

Before cooking, place the panko-coated, raw nuggets on a parchment-lined baking sheet, freeze them for an hour, then put them in labeled zip-top bags and freeze for up to 4 months. When ready to eat, cook as directed, adding 2 minutes to the cooking time.

Dijon, Honey, and Garlic Hasselback Chicken Breast

4 skinless, boneless chicken breasts

Kosher salt and freshly ground black pepper

3 tablespoons unsalted butter

4 cloves garlic, chopped

3 tablespoons Dijon or grainy mustard

¼ cup (60 ml) honey

Hot tip for whenever you have friends coming over: If the smell of warm butter and garlic is emanating from your kitchen, people will immediately assume you're a genius chef. If you're not familiar with the term "hasselback," it means to slice through a food to create fan-like slices. Potatoes are most popular for this technique, but if you're not doing it with chicken, now is the time to start. This recipe is a truly unique way to make chicken, because of the way it's sliced; bathed in a garlic, honey, Dijon mixture, and then baked, so the edges of the chicken crisp while every bite remains moist. It's a gorgeous dish—"fancy" in appearance and absolutely decadent in taste, while also being one of the simplest recipes in the book.

+ Preheat the oven to 425°F (220°C).

+ Take a sharp knife and, on a slight diagonal, make six evenly spaced cuts into each chicken breast, going about 75 percent of the way through. Season the chicken breasts all over with salt and pepper.

+ In a medium sauté pan, melt the butter over low to medium heat. Add the garlic and sauté for 30 seconds. You don't want it to brown. Whisk in the Dijon mustard and honey and cook for 1 to 2 minutes, or until it's thoroughly combined with the butter.

+ Place the chicken breasts on a parchment- or foil-lined baking sheet or pan. Pour the honey Dijon mixture over the top of the chicken breasts, making sure to coat inside the slits. Bake for 22 to 25 minutes. Turn on the broiler and cook for an additional 1 to 2 minutes, or until the tops are golden and bubbly.

Play around with different types of mustard in this recipe, from Dijon to a grainy mustard. It will even work with ordinary yellow mustard.

Don't have chicken breasts? This recipe works great with skinless, boneless chicken thighs and thick salmon fillets too.

TO ENJOY LATER
The cooked chicken can be cooled and then stored in an airtight container in the refrigerator for up to 3 days.

PREP IN ADVANCE
Make the marinade up to 3 days ahead and store it in an airtight container in the refrigerator.

REPURPOSE LEFTOVERS
Chop the chicken into cubes and toss with salad greens, cooked rice, quinoa, or vegetables.

The BEST Chicken Burger

1½ pounds (680 g) ground chicken

1 cup (30 g) finely chopped fresh spinach

1 teaspoon garlic powder

½ teaspoon onion powder

½ teaspoon dried thyme, mixed Italian herbs, or sage

½ teaspoon paprika

1 teaspoon kosher salt

Freshly ground black pepper

1 tablespoon olive oil

4 to 6 hamburger buns, toasted

Optional toppings: sliced avocado, mayonnaise, ketchup, mustard, lettuce, sliced tomato, raw or sautéed onions

I have a secret for you, but you must promise to keep it to yourself: Fresh spinach is what makes these chicken burgers magnificently moist. Additionally, for anyone in your house who is averse to greens, they won't taste the spinach at all. This recipe also avoids the need for breadcrumbs or other fillers, making these burgers naturally gluten-free. Sandwich them in your go-to burger bun, or if you want to double down on the health benefits, wrap each burger in lettuce for a super satisfying, carb-free meal.

✦ In a large bowl, add the chicken, spinach, garlic powder, onion powder, thyme, paprika, salt, and pepper. Using your hands, mix the ingredients until combined and form into 4 to 6 large patties.

✦ Heat a large sauté pan or grill pan over medium heat. Add the oil and place the patties in the pan. Cook the burgers for 4 minutes on each side, or until lightly golden and cooked through.

✦ Place a patty on each bottom bun, add any of your desired toppings, and then top with the second part of the bun.

You'll get a super tender patty with even more flavor in each bite by visiting your spice drawer. Feel free to add a teaspoon of any spice you love, such as harissa, Italian herbs, smoked paprika, or chile flakes.

TO ENJOY LATER
The cooked burgers can be cooled and refrigerated up to 3 days. To rewarm, microwave for 30 seconds, or place in a saucepan over low to medium heat for 1 to 2 minutes on each side, or in an air fryer at 350°F (175°C) for 2 minutes, or until warmed through.

PREP IN ADVANCE
The uncooked burgers can be placed on parchment-lined baking sheets, frozen for 1 hour, and then placed in labeled zip-top bags. Defrost in a refrigerator overnight and then cook as directed.

REPURPOSE LEFTOVERS
Crumble the cooked burgers over rice (or other favorite grain), or wrap them in lettuce for a carb-free meal.

Liquid Gold Chicken Stock

PREP TIME
10 minutes

COOK TIME
3 hours

MAKES
4 quarts (3.8 liters)

1½ pounds (680 g) chicken drumsticks

2 small yellow onions, skin-on, quartered

4 medium carrots, not peeled, roughly chopped

4 small parsnips, not peeled, roughly chopped

4 stalks celery, roughly chopped

1 head garlic, halved through the cloves

1 bunch fresh parsley stems

¼ cup (70 g) whole black peppercorns

Combining just a handful of inexpensive ingredients, you can churn out a giant, nutritious batch of this liquid gold. It's a lovely base for myriad soups, or perfect for sipping on its own whenever you feel a bit under the weather. I like using the Instant Pot for speed, but your stovetop works well too.

✦ Preheat the oven to 450°F (230°C). Add the chicken drumsticks, onions, carrots, parsnips, celery, and garlic to a large, rimmed sheet pan. Roast for 1 hour, or until the chicken is golden and the vegetables are dark brown. Add 2 cups (480 ml) water to the sheet pan and cook for 10 minutes more.

✦ Carefully remove the pan from the oven. Using tongs, transfer the solids to the pot of a 6-quart (5.7 liter) electric pressure cooker. Pour the liquid into the pot, including any brown bits that have collected on the sheet pan.

✦ Add the parsley stems and peppercorns to the pot, then fill with cold water to the max fill line designated on the pressure cooker (about 18 cups/4.3 liters water). Place the lid on with the vent set to "seal." Cook on high pressure for 1 hour. Let the pressure release naturally for 15 minutes, then manually release the remaining pressure. *(Alternatively, if making on the stovetop: Place the ingredients, including the same amount of water as above, in a large stockpot, bring to a boil with the lid ajar, reduce heat to the lowest simmer, skimming the foam off the top occasionally, and cook for 1½ hours or until the chicken is cooked through. Or, if using a slow cooker: After the bones roast, place all of the ingredients in the slow cooker, with the same amount of water, on low for 8 hours.)*

✦ Strain the stock through a fine-mesh strainer. If freezing, store in freezer-safe 1-quart (about 1 liter) containers, leaving some space at the top so the stock can expand when it freezes.

This is a stock, not a broth. Stock is made without seasoning because it is usually cooked down. If it starts seasoned, it usually becomes too salty once it's reduced. Broth, on the other hand, is seasoned when made, so if you'd prefer to turn this recipe into a broth, simply season it to taste after straining.

Replace the store-bought chicken or vegetable stock called for in Classic Chicken Soup (page 89), Turkey and Quinoa Chili (page 103), Wild Rice and Mushroom Soup (page 195), or any other recipes in this book with this all-purpose stock.

TO ENJOY LATER

Allow the stock to cool, then refrigerate in an airtight container for up to 4 days. To freeze, cool and divide the stock between glass jars or freezer bags filled three-quarters full, so they can expand. Use for up to 4 months. Alternatively, the broth can be divided into ice cube trays, frozen, and then removed from the trays and placed in labeled zip-top bags.

PREP IN ADVANCE

Instead of throwing away the vegetable scraps, place them in a zip-top bag and store it in the freezer, adding to it over the month. Make stock when you have several cups worth.

REPURPOSE LEFTOVERS

Remove the chicken meat from the drumsticks to add to your Freezer-Stash Breakfast Burritos (page 66), Wild Mushroom Bean Bowl (page 160), or a green salad dressed with Creamy Balsamic Vinaigrette (page 128).

Classic Chicken Soup

PREP TIME
10 minutes

COOK TIME
3 hours

MAKES
4 quarts (3.8 liters)

2 tablespoons olive oil

1 small onion, diced

4 carrots, peeled and thinly sliced

4 small parsnips, peeled and thinly sliced

4 stalks celery, thinly sliced

3 quarts (12 cups/2.8 liters) Liquid Gold Chicken Stock (page 86)

Kosher salt and freshly ground black pepper

2 boneless, skinless chicken breasts (about 1 pound/455 g)

8 ounces (225 g) cooked pasta, or 2 cups (390 g) cooked rice, for serving

½ cup (25 g) chopped fresh flat- or curley-leaf parsley, for serving

My oldest daughter would eat this classic chicken soup everyday if she could. As a result, I keep jars of it on hand in our freezer year-round. My secret ingredient is the parsnips. They add a lovely depth of flavor to the soup, as well as a slight sweetness. After all these years of making it, I've got it down to what feels like a science.

◆ Heat the olive oil in a large stockpot or Dutch oven over medium heat for 1 minute, then add onion, carrots, parsnips, and celery. Sauté for 5 to 7 minutes, or until the onions start to become translucent and the carrots and parsnips start to soften.

◆ Add the stock and a very generous pinch of salt and pepper. Bring to a boil, then reduce the heat to a simmer.

◆ Add the chicken breasts and cook for 20 minutes, or until cooked through (an instant-read thermometer inserted into the chicken should register 165°F / 75°C).

◆ Remove the chicken from the soup and shred with two forks. Return the shredded chicken to the pot and stir in the cooked pasta. Add the chopped parsley and taste and adjust the seasoning before serving.

If you prefer, you can simply toss leftover shredded chicken into the soup once the vegetables are tender instead of poaching the chicken in the soup.

TO ENJOY LATER

If I am not serving the soup right away, I like to wait to add the cooked pasta or rice. Let the soup cool and then refrigerate for up to 4 days. Or to freeze, cool and divide the soup among glass jars or freezer bags filled three-quarters full so they can expand when frozen. Rewarm the soup in the microwave or in a pot over low to medium heat. Pour it over cooked pasta or rice, if desired, and sprinkle with the fresh parsley.

Crispy Chicken Thighs

with ARTICHOKES, LEMON, AND HERBS

8 bone-in, skin-on chicken thighs

Kosher salt and freshly ground black pepper

1 tablespoon olive oil

1 shallot, thinly sliced

1 (12-ounce/340 g) bag frozen artichoke hearts, or 1 (14-ounce/400 g) can quartered artichoke hearts, drained

½ cup (120 ml) dry white wine

1 cup (240 ml) Liquid Gold Chicken Stock (page 86)

1 tablespoon Dijon mustard

Juice from ½ lemon

½ cup (25 g) chopped fresh flat- or curly-leaf parsley

This may just become your new favorite weeknight dinner. If you prefer breast meat, allow me to recite some ways that thighs are superior. Chicken thighs are a much more flavorful, economical, and forgiving cut of chicken to cook; they don't dry out nearly as easily, making them perfect for braising and grilling. Enough of my counting, see for yourself!

✦ Preheat the oven to 350°F (175°C). Pat the chicken thighs dry with a paper towel, then season liberally on both sides with salt and pepper.

✦ Heat the olive oil in a large ovenproof skillet over medium-high heat. Once the oil is shimmering, add half of the chicken thighs skin side down and cook undisturbed for 6 to 8 minutes, or until the skin is deeply golden. Flip over and cook for an additional 5 minutes on the other side. Remove from heat and set aside on a large plate. Repeat with the remaining chicken thighs.

✦ Once all of the chicken has been browned, to the same pan, add the shallot and cook over medium heat for 2 to 3 minutes, or until softened and fragrant. Add the artichoke hearts and cook, stirring occasionally, for 6 to 8 minutes. Pour in the wine to deglaze, stirring to loosen any brown bits that have formed on the bottom of the pan. Let the wine come to a boil, then reduce the heat to a simmer for 2 minutes.

✦ Add the chicken stock and mustard and whisk to combine, then bring to a boil. Season with salt and pepper, then return the chicken thighs to the pan, skin side up. Bake in the preheated oven for 20 minutes, or until the thighs are cooked through (165°F/75°C on an instant-read thermometer).

✦ Remove from the oven and squeeze the fresh lemon juice over the top, then sprinkle with the fresh parsley before serving.

This same cooking method can be used with a ton of different flavor combinations. One favorite is blistered tomato. Just swap the artichokes for 1 pint (290 g) cherry tomatoes—or whatever ingredient you might be craving, fresh or frozen, including summer squash slices, butternut squash or potato cubes, and/or carrot coins.

TO ENJOY LATER

The chicken can be cooled and then refrigerated in an airtight container for up to 3 days.

REPURPOSE LEFTOVERS

Chop any remaining chicken meat and mix with the remaining artichokes, sauce, and any cherry tomatoes or leftover cooked vegetables you have on hand in your kitchen. Place in small ramekins, top with mozzarella, and bake for 15 minutes in a 350°F (175°C) oven or until cheese is melted and bubbly.

Lemon-Pepper Spatchcock Roast Chicken

with POTATOES AND ONIONS

1 roasting chicken
(3½ to 4 pounds/1.6
to 1.8 kg), giblets
removed and
discarded, patted dry

2 tablespoons olive oil

2 small onions, thinly
sliced

5 medium potatoes
(about 2 pounds/910 g),
scrubbed and cut into
1-inch (2.5 cm) chunks

2 teaspoons lemon
pepper (no salt added)

Kosher salt and freshly
ground black pepper

Fresh thyme sprigs, for
garnish

Spatchcock is just a fancy way of describing a whole chicken sans backbone. What is the point of that? First, it cooks faster. Second, flattening the bird allows the chicken to cook evenly, so the breast meat and dark meat will be ready at the same time. Last, it results in more surface area, thus maximum crispy skin. I often will roast a second chicken while I'm at it and use the leftover chicken for other meals later in the week.

✦ Preheat the oven to 450°F (230°C). While the oven preheats, prepare your chicken. Place the whole chicken breast side down on a cutting board. Using sharp kitchen shears, cut down each side of the backbone, then remove and discard it (or set aside to make stock). Flip the chicken over and tuck the wings back, hooking the tips behind the wing joint. Using your hands, apply strong force to the center of the breastbone to flatten the bird into one even layer. Set aside at room temperature.

✦ Add 1 tablespoon olive oil to a sturdy rimmed sheet pan. Add the onions and potatoes, 1 teaspoon of the lemon pepper, and a pinch of salt and black pepper to taste. Toss to combine. Roast for 15 minutes, or until the onions and potatoes begin to soften.

✦ Remove the sheet pan from the oven and push the potatoes and onions away from the center. Place the chicken in the center of the pan, then drizzle with the remaining tablespoon olive oil. Add the remaining teaspoon lemon pepper and a generous pinch of salt and black pepper, and rub the seasoning into the chicken until evenly coated.

✦ Return to the oven to roast for 45 to 50 minutes, or until the chicken is golden and an instant-read thermometer inserted into the thickest part of the thigh registers 165°F (75°C).

✦ Remove the pan from the oven and tent the chicken with foil. Let rest for 10 minutes. When cool enough to handle, carve the chicken, first removing the legs and wings with a sharp knife, and then slicing the breast meat. Serve alongside the roasted potatoes and onions.

I promise, removing the backbone is an easy job, but if it gives you the chills, have your butcher do it. Also, some specialty grocers sell chickens that have already been flattened!

Feel like switching up the flavors? Try this same recipe Cajun-style by swapping the lemon pepper for your favorite Cajun seasoning blend and swapping the potatoes for three bell peppers, cut into strips.

Have some fresh herbs on hand? Add some fresh rosemary or thyme sprigs in or around the chicken while it roasts.

TO ENJOY LATER
The chicken and vegetables can be cooled and then stored in an airtight container in the refrigerator for up to 3 days.

REPURPOSE LEFTOVERS
Finely chop any leftovers to put into a tortilla or place over salad greens tossed with Creamy Balsamic Vinaigrette (page 128) for lunch the next day. Also, consider reserving any leftover chicken parts, in particular the backbone, to make chicken stock (page 86). Just toss any scraps in to roast along with the chicken legs called for in the stock recipe. Not ready to make stock right now? Place the parts in a zip-top bag and freeze for a rainy day.

Sheet-Pan Sausage and Peppers

3 red, orange, green, or yellow bell peppers, cut into wedges

1 large yellow onion, cut into wedges

4 cloves garlic, smashed and peeled

2 tablespoons olive oil

1 teaspoon kosher salt

Freshly ground black pepper

1 (12-ounce/340 g) package turkey or chicken sausage, cut into 1-inch (2.5 cm) pieces

Fresh basil and/or shaved Parmesan cheese, for serving

This recipe is a culinary ode to my oldest daughter, who I have long referred to as "my little carnivore." She's never come across a steak, chicken, slab of bacon, or especially sausage that she didn't want to inhale. Years ago, she had sausage with peppers and onions for dinner at a friend's house and proceeded to reminisce about it incessantly. After a year, I finally made it for her. This sheet pan dinner is one of the most delicious, simplest chop, toss, and roast recipes you can imagine—and the bonus? There's only a cutting board, knife, and sheet pan to clean. Don't stress about what kind of sausage to use: kielbasa, chicken apple, sweet and spicy turkey, andouille, bratwurst, or anything you love. And feel free to add other ingredients too. For instance, if you have a handful of cherry tomatoes, toss them onto the pan with the other vegetables.

✦ Preheat the oven to 425°F (220°C). Place the bell peppers, onions, and garlic on a large sheet pan lined with parchment paper. Drizzle everything with the olive oil and sprinkle with salt and black pepper. Use your hands to toss to coat evenly. Place the sheet pan in the oven and bake for 10 minutes.

✦ Place the sausage on the sheet pan, spacing it out in between the vegetables, and roast for an additional 25 minutes, or until the vegetables are fork tender, the sausages are golden, and both are cooked through. *(Alternatively, to cook this dish in an air fryer: Simply place all of the ingredients in the basket, toss to coat, and cook at 400°F [205°C] for 20 minutes, or until the peppers are golden and the sausage is cooked through.)*

We love this on its own, but it's also delicious divided into 6 hoagie rolls.

For easier cleanup, I like to line the sheet pan with parchment paper before placing the vegetables and sausage on to roast.

TO ENJOY LATER

This can be cooled and refrigerated in an airtight container for up to 3 days. Reheat in the microwave for 1 to 2 minutes or until heated through.

REPURPOSE LEFTOVERS

Chop any leftover sausage and peppers into bite-size pieces. Stir into cooked pasta, drizzle with olive oil, and heat for 1 to 2 minutes in the microwave or in a small saucepan or until heated through. Sprinkle generously with Parmesan cheese to taste.

Sausage and Kale Soup

PREP TIME
15 minutes

COOK TIME
45 minutes

SERVES
4

1 tablespoon olive oil

1 pound (455 g) chorizo sausage links (or your preferred sausage), cut into ¼-inch (6 mm) slices

1 onion, diced

Kosher salt and freshly ground black pepper

Crushed red pepper

4 cloves garlic, thinly sliced

4 medium Yukon gold potatoes (about 1½ pounds/680 g), cut into 1-inch (25 cm) cubes

6 cups (1.4 L) Liquid Gold Chicken Stock (page 86)

2 (15-ounce/430 g) cans cannellini beans, drained and rinsed

2 bunches lacinato kale, cleaned, stems discarded, leaves roughly chopped

Are you craving something to warm you up from the inside out? Look no further than this humble, flavor-packed soup. You'll be amazed how easily you can transform just a few simple ingredients into one of the best soups you've ever had. This recipe is inspired by caldo verde, a classic Portuguese dish full of chorizo (a smoked, spiced sausage), kale, and potatoes. I love the flavor that chorizo lends to this recipe, but any style of sausage (even plant-based!) will work well in this recipe. This soup is a crowd-pleaser, so make sure to double the recipe so you can freeze some for later, and don't forget to serve it with some crusty bread.

✦ Heat the oil in a large Dutch oven or heavy-bottomed pot over medium heat. Once shimmering, add the sausage and cook, stirring occasionally, until browned, 4 to 5 minutes. Remove the sausage pieces from the pot with a slotted spoon and set aside.

✦ To the same pot over medium heat, add the onion and a pinch of salt, black pepper, and crushed red pepper. Cook, stirring often, until the onions begin to soften and turn translucent, 5 to 7 minutes. Add the garlic and potatoes and cook just until the garlic is fragrant, 2 minutes. Return the browned sausage to the pot, then add the chicken stock and season with salt and black pepper. Bring to a boil, then reduce heat to a simmer and cook for 20 minutes, or until the potatoes are tender.

✦ Add the beans and kale to the soup and cook for 5 minutes, or until the beans are warmed through and the kale has wilted and is tender. Season to taste and serve.

Think of this recipe as a blank canvas. I use kale, but collard greens or Swiss chard work just as well. Same goes for the beans—I like the creaminess white beans add, but red kidney beans or chickpeas are A-OK, too!

TO ENJOY LATER
The soup can be cooled and refrigerated in an airtight container for up to 4 days. Or to freeze, cool and divide the soup among glass jars or freezer bags filled three-quarters full so they can expand. Rewarm the soup in the microwave or in a pot over low to medium heat and pour over leftover pasta, rice, or your favorite grain, if desired.

PREP TIME
15 minutes, plus 1 to 2
hours for marinating

COOK TIME
15 minutes

SERVES
4 to 6

Grilled Pork Tenderloin
with CHIMICHURRI

¼ cup (60 ml) Dijon
mustard

½ cup (120 ml) apple
cider vinegar

3 tablespoons light or
dark brown sugar

8 cloves garlic, minced

⅓ cup (75 ml) plus 2
tablespoons olive oil

1½ teaspoons kosher
salt

2 to 2½ pounds
(910 g to 1.2 kg) pork
tenderloin, fat and
silver skin removed

½ cup (15 g) packed
fresh cilantro

½ cup (15 g) packed
flat- or curly-leaf
parsley

1 small shallot, peeled

2 tablespoons red or
white wine vinegar

2 tablespoons fresh
lime juice

Pinch crushed red
pepper

Freshly ground black
pepper

It was in Argentina where I began my love affair with chimichurri; a pot of it accompanied whatever meat we were eating. Just the thought of pairing it with pork tenderloin makes me giddy.

✦ Place the Dijon mustard, apple cider vinegar, brown sugar, half of the garlic, 2 tablespoons of the olive oil, and 1 teaspoon salt in a large zip-top bag. Squish the bag to mix the marinade. Add the pork tenderloin and use your hand on the outside of the bag to move the marinade around the pork. Marinate for 1 to hours at room temperature or overnight in the refrigerator.

✦ To make the chimichurri, in a food processor, place the cilantro, parsley, remaining garlic, shallot, the remaining ⅓ cup (75 ml) olive oil, the red or white wine vinegar, lime juice, crushed red pepper, remaining ½ teaspoon salt, and black pepper and pulse until finely chopped.

✦ Heat a grill to medium heat. Grill the marinated pork on several sides for a total of 14 to 15 minutes, or until the internal temperature is 135 to 140°F (55 to 60°C) when checked with an instant-read thermometer inserted in the thickest part of the meat. (*Alternatively, you can use a cast-iron skillet to roast the pork. Heat over medium-high heat and add 1 tablespoon of olive oil. Sear the pork all over for a total of 6 minutes. Transfer the pan to a 400°F (205°C) oven and roast for 15 to 20 minutes.*)

✦ Allow the pork to rest for at least 10 minutes to allow the juices to settle before slicing. Use a sharp knife to cut pork on a bias into ½-inch (12 mm) slices and top with the chimichurri sauce.

Make sure not to overcook the pork. Pork should never be cooked to more than 135 to 140°F (55 to 60°C). You want the internal color to be light pink.

Make double the amount of chimichurri sauce to serve with fish, shrimp, chicken, or steak later that week.

TO ENJOY LATER
The cooked pork can be cooled and refrigerated in an airtight container for up to 3 days. Enjoy at room temperature or warm for 30 seconds in the microwave. Store the chimichurri in an airtight container in the fridge for up to 5 days, or freeze in ice cube trays then transfer to labeled zip-top bags for up to 4 months.

PREP IN ADVANCE
Place the zip-top bag of the pork in its marinade in the freezer for up to 3 months. When ready to cook, place the pork chops in the zip-top bag in the refrigerator to thaw overnight; cook as directed.

PREP TIME
20 minutes

COOK TIME
Air-fried: 12 minutes;
pan-fried: 4 minutes

SERVES
4

Succulent Boneless Pork Chops

1½ pounds (680 g) thinly sliced, boneless pork chops (about 8)

1 teaspoon kosher salt, plus more as needed

1 teaspoon paprika

1 teaspoon dried minced garlic

½ teaspoon freshly ground black pepper

½ cup (65 g) all-purpose flour

2 large eggs, beaten

1½ cups (150 g) seasoned breadcrumbs

Cooking spray, if air frying, or olive oil, if panfrying

This recipe turns out pork chops that are moist and succulent on the inside and super crisp on the outside. I prefer to use the air fryer but your stovetop will work!

✦ Pat the pork chops dry with a paper towel. In a small bowl, combine the salt, paprika, minced garlic, and pepper. Season both sides of the pork with the spice mixture, reserving the excess.

✦ Add the flour to a large plate or shallow bowl and mix in the excess spice mixture. Add the beaten eggs to a separate shallow bowl, and place the breadcrumbs in a third large plate or shallow bowl. Working with one pork chop at a time, coat in flour, tapping off excess. Then, coat in egg, letting the excess drip off before covering both sides of the chop with seasoned breadcrumbs. Set aside on a plate, then repeat the breading process with the remaining pork.

✦ If using the air fryer, spray both sides of the pork lightly with cooking spray. Place however many chops will fit in an even layer in the air-fryer basket and cook for 12 minutes. Remove from the air fryer when golden and the pork reaches at least 145°F (65°C) on an instant-read thermometer. *(Alternatively, if you wish to panfry the pork, add about ¼ inch [6 mm] olive oil to a wide, deep sauté pan set over medium heat. Once the oil is shimmering, add the pork chops in an even layer and cook for about 2 minutes per side, or until golden, and the pork reaches at least 145°F [65°C] on an instant-read thermometer.)* Season with kosher salt and serve hot.

The total cooking time will depend on the size of your air fryer or sauté pan. You want the pork chops to be in an even layer while cooking, so you may need to cook them in a few batches. As you finish cooking the pork chops, place them on a cooking rack or foil-lined baking sheet in a 250°F (120°C) oven for up to 20 minutes to keep warm.

My favorite way to serve these is with apple sauce!

PREP IN ADVANCE
After breading pork chops, place chops on a plate and cover for up to 24 hours before cooking.

REPURPOSE LEFTOVERS
Leftover pork chops can be diced and placed on favorite salad greens or vegetables and topped with Creamy Balsamic Vinaigrette (page 128).

PREP TIME
15 minutes

COOK TIME
45 minutes

SERVES
6 to 8

Turkey and Quinoa Chili

2 tablespoons olive oil

1 large onion, diced

2 carrots, peeled and diced

1 bell pepper, diced

3 cloves garlic, minced

2 pounds (910 g) ground turkey

1 tablespoon ground cumin

2 teaspoons chili powder*

1 teaspoon kosher salt

Freshly ground black pepper

1 (28-ounce/795 g) can diced tomatoes with juices

1 (4-ounce) can green chiles

2 (15-ounce/430 g) cans beans

4 cups (one 32-ounce/960 ml box) chicken broth or Liquid Gold Chicken Stock (page 86)

½ cup (85 g) uncooked quinoa

I usually cook this recipe on the stovetop in a big pot, but a slow cooker or Instant Pot works great too. The flavors will only continue to get better and better the longer it cooks. Like all chili, this freezes well, so consider making a double batch.

✦ In a large pot over medium heat, add the olive oil and onions and cook for 3 to 4 minutes. Add the carrots and bell pepper and sauté for 2 to 3 minutes, or until they start to soften. Add the garlic, turkey, cumin, chili powder, salt, and black pepper and saute for 4 to 5 minutes or until turkey begins to cook through, breaking it up into small pieces with a wooden spoon as it cooks. Then, add the diced tomatoes, chiles, beans, and the broth.

✦ Bring to a boil, reduce to a simmer, and cook covered for at least 25 minutes and preferably up to 50 minutes to allow time for the flavors to really meld together. *(Alternatively, if using a slow cooker, in a large sauté pan, sauté the onion, carrots, bell pepper, and garlic as directed above. Transfer to the slower cooker, add the rest of the ingredients, seal tightly, and cook on low for 4 to 8 hours or on high for 2 to 4 hours. If using an Instant Pot, turn the pot to sauté, add the olive oil, and cook the vegetables for 3 minutes. Add the turkey and cook 3 minutes more. Add the remaining ingredients, cover with the lid, and set to the chili/bean setting. Cook for 20 minutes and then release the pressure.)*

I keep the chili powder at 2 teaspoons when my kids are eating it, but if it's adults only, add 1 tablespoon (or even more if you're feeling adventurous).

I like using one can of kidney and one can of white or navy beans but anything you have on hand will work.

TO ENJOY LATER

The chili can be cooled and then refrigerated in an airtight container for up to 4 days. To freeze, cool and divide among glass jars or freezer bags filled three-quarters full, so they can expand when frozen for up to 4 months. Rewarm the chili in the microwave or on the stovetop over low to medium heat. Pour over leftover pasta, rice, or another favorite grain, if desired.

PREP TIME
15 minutes

COOK TIME
3 hours

SERVES
4 to 6

Italian Braised Beef

2 pounds (910 g) chuck roast, fat trimmed, cut into 2-inch (5 cm) cubes

Kosher salt and freshly ground black pepper

1 teaspoon dried basil

1 teaspoon dried oregano

1 teaspoon fennel seeds

1 teaspoon garlic powder

1 tablespoon canola oil

1 tablespoon olive oil

1 onion, chopped

4 stalks celery, chopped

3 medium carrots, diced

4 cloves garlic, thinly sliced

2 tablespoons tomato paste

1 cup (240 ml) red wine

1 (28-ounce/795 g) can crushed tomatoes

FOR SERVING
Cooked pasta or polenta, prepared according to the package instructions

Freshly grated Parmesan cheese

Chopped fresh flat- or curly-leaf parsley

Think of this recipe as a deeply flavored ragù crossed with a stew. Pure heaven.

✦ Preheat the oven to 325°F (165°C). Pat the beef cubes dry. In a small bowl, combine 2 teaspoons salt, 1 teaspoon pepper, basil, oregano, fennel seeds, and garlic powder. Evenly coat the beef in the seasoning mix.

✦ In a large Dutch oven, heat the canola oil over medium heat. Once shimmering, sear half of the beef until deeply browned, about 5 to 6 minutes. Remove with a slotted spoon and set aside. Repeat with the remaining beef.

✦ Once all the beef has been browned, discard the canola oil, reserving any brown bits that have collected on the bottom of the pot. Heat the olive oil in the pot over medium heat. Once shimmering, add the onion, celery, and carrots and cook for 8 minutes, or until they begin to soften. Add the garlic and cook, about 1 minute. Add the tomato paste and cook for 1 to 2 minutes, then add the wine and deglaze, scraping up any brown bits that have collected on the bottom of the pot. Cook until the liquid is reduced by half, about 3 minutes.

✦ Add the crushed tomatoes and 1 cup (120 ml) water. Bring to a boil, then return the beef to the pot and reduce to a simmer. Season with salt and pepper, then roast in the preheated oven for 2 to 2½ hours, or until the beef is very tender. Remove the beef from the pot and shred into bite-size pieces to make it thicker, if des

ired. Return the beef to the pot, stirring to combine. If the ragù is thicker than you prefer, thin it with 1 to 2 cups (120 to 240 ml) water and simmer for 5 to 10 minutes more. *(Alternatively, sear the meat right in the pressure cooker, then add the remaining ingredients and cook at high pressure for 40 minutes. Let the pressure release manually, then shred beef and serve. Another alternative: After sautéing the meat, you can place it and the remaining ingredients in a slow cooker on low heat for 8 hours or until fork tender.)*

✦ Serve over warm pasta or cooked polenta. Garnish with the Parmesan cheese and chopped parsley.

TO ENJOY LATER
The beef can be cooled and then refrigerated in an airtight container for up to 3 days.

PREP IN ADVANCE
The day before, the seasoning mix can be made and the vegetables can be chopped and refrigerated to speed up the prep time.

PREP TIME
15 minutes plus 1 hour
for freezing

COOK TIME
15 minutes

SERVES
4

Buffalo Tofu

with RANCH DIP

1 (14-ounce/400 g)
block extra-firm tofu

½ cup (65 g) cornstarch

½ cup (120 ml)
unflavored plant-
based milk

1 cup (85 g) panko or
breadcrumbs

½ teaspoon garlic
powder

¼ teaspoon onion
powder

½ teaspoon paprika

Kosher salt and freshly
ground black pepper

3 to 4 tablespoons
vegetable oil (for pan-
frying the tofu)

½ cup (120 ml) prepared
Buffalo sauce

Nonstick cooking spray

RANCH DIP
¾ cup (180 ml) vegan
mayonnaise

3 tablespoons
unflavored plant-
based milk

2 teaspoons fresh
lemon juice or apple
cider vinegar

½ teaspoon each of
dried dill, dried chives,
dried parsley, garlic
powder

Kosher salt and freshly
ground black pepper

These super crunchy bites should enter the Buffalo Hall of Fame. Try 'em and see.

✦ Wrap the tofu in a kitchen towel and place something heavy on top for 10 minutes to remove excess liquid.

✦ Cut the tofu lengthwise into 1-inch (2.5 cm) cubes. Place on a parchment-lined plate or a sheet pan and freeze for 1 hour or overnight. This helps give the tofu a firmer, meatier texture. Place the cornstarch in a zip-top bag or bowl and add the tofu cubes. Toss to coat completely.

✦ Place the milk in a medium-size shallow bowl. In another medium-size shallow bowl, stir together the panko, garlic and onion powders, paprika, 1 teaspoon salt, and some pepper. Using a fork and working in batches, place the cornstarch-coated tofu in the milk first and then into the panko mixture to coat all sides.

✦ Using tongs or your fingers, place the tofu cubes in an air-fryer basket and spritz them with cooking spray to coat evenly. Air fry the tofu at 400°F (205°C) for 10 minutes or until the tofu is starting to turn golden. *(Alternatively, the tofu can be sauteed in a thin layer of oil in a pan over medium heat for 5 to 6 minutes, shaking the pan so the tofu turns golden on each side.)*

✦ Meanwhile, make the dip: Add the mayonnaise, milk, lemon juice, dill, garlic powder, chives, parsley, ¼ teaspoon salt, and some black pepper to a bowl and stir to combine.

✦ Place the buffalo sauce in a medium bowl and add the fried tofu, stirring to coat. Return the tofu to the air fryer for 5 more minutes, or until golden outside.

✦ Serve the crispy tofu bites with the ranch dip.

If you've got a head of romaine, you've got a killer vegan Buffalo tofu salad. Thinly chop your lettuce, top with crispy tofu, and drizzle with the Ranch Dip, adding a few more tablespoons of milk to turn the dip into more of a salad dressing.

The recipe calls for plant-based milk and vegan mayonnaise but feel free to substitute with cow's milk and standard mayo, if you aren't vegan.

PREP IN ADVANCE
Place the tofu cubes on a parchment-lined baking sheet and freeze for 1 hour or up to overnight. Place in labeled zip-top bags for up to 3 months. The sauce can be prepared, stored in an airtight container, and refrigerated for up to 2 days before using.

Miso Asparagus Sheet-Pan Tofu

⅓ cup (75 ml) olive oil, plus more for the pan

2 tablespoons white miso paste

2 cloves garlic, minced

Juice of 1 lemon

1 (14-ounce/400 g) block extra-firm tofu, pressed, cut into ¼-inch (6 mm) planks

Freshly ground black pepper

1 bunch asparagus, woody ends trimmed and discarded, cut into 1-inch (2.5 cm) segments

Cooked quinoa or steamed rice, for serving

Something almost spiritual happens when miso paste, olive oil, garlic, and lemon come together. Really. The glaze for this tofu is SO insanely yummy, I advise you to make a double batch because you'll want to slather it on everything!

✦ Preheat the oven to 450°F (230°C). Coat a rimmed sheet pan with olive oil.

✦ To make the glaze, pour the olive oil into a large, microwave-safe measuring cup or bowl. Heat for 15 to 30 seconds in the microwave, or just until the oil is warm to the touch. *(Alternatively, the olive oil can be placed in a small saucepan set over medium heat and warmed for one minute.)*

✦ Whisk in the miso, garlic, and lemon juice, mixing until emulsified and smooth. Add the pressed tofu planks to the prepared sheet pan. Season each side with pepper, then brush the tops with the prepared miso glaze. Roast for 15 minutes, or until the miso glaze starts to turn golden and caramelize on the edges.

✦ Remove the pan from the oven and flip the tofu over. Brush with more miso glaze, then toss the asparagus with the remaining glaze before adding the coated pieces to the sheet pan.

✦ Roast for an additional 15 minutes, or until the asparagus is tender and the tofu is golden and starting to caramelize on the edges. Serve with quinoa.

PREP IN ADVANCE

Chop the asparagus, press and cut the tofu, prepare the glaze, and then refrigerate, so that you can quickly assemble the ingredients and roast up to 24 hours later.

Sheet-Pan BBQ Tofu
with ROASTED CORN AND TOMATO

1 teaspoon smoked paprika

½ teaspoon kosher salt, plus more as needed

Pinch cayenne

Freshly ground black pepper

1 (14-ounce/400 g) block extra-firm tofu, pressed, cut into ¼-inch (6 mm) planks

1 tablespoon olive oil

1 pint (290 g) cherry tomatoes, halved

2 cups fresh or frozen corn kernels, thawed if frozen

¼ cup (60 ml) prepared barbeque sauce

FOR SERVING
Steamed rice

Lime wedges

Roughly chopped fresh cilantro (leaves and stems)

This is the ideal weeknight dinner to throw together, especially when your garden is bursting with cherry tomatoes! Using a sweet, sticky BBQ sauce allows the tofu to get deliciously crisp and caramelized.

✦ Preheat the oven to 425°F (220°C).

✦ In a small bowl, combine the smoked paprika, salt, cayenne, and a few grinds of black pepper. Sprinkle the spice mixture all over both sides of the pressed tofu planks.

✦ Coat the sheet pan with the olive oil, then place the seasoned tofu on top, leaving space between each plank. Scatter the tomatoes and corn around the tofu. Season everything with salt and pepper. Roast for 20 minutes, then flip the tofu over and roast for 20 more minutes, or until the tomatoes start to burst and the corn is beginning to caramelize. Remove the pan from the oven, brush the tops of the tofu with barbecue sauce, then flip the planks over and brush the other side.

✦ Reset the oven to the high broil function. Once hot, place the sheet pan under the broiler and brown the tofu for 1 to 2 minutes per side, or until the barbecue sauce starts to caramelize. Keep a close eye on the tofu as it can quickly burn.

✦ Serve over steamed rice with a squeeze of fresh lime and a handful of fresh cilantro.

PREP IN ADVANCE
The entire dish can be assembled on the baking sheet, covered, and then refrigerated for up to 24 hours in advance and then roasted as directed.

PREP TIME
15 minutes

COOK TIME
45 minutes

SERVES
2 to 4

Spicy Squash and Broccoli Rabe Sheet-Pan Tofu

3 tablespoons olive oil, plus more for the pan

1 (14-ounce/400 g) block extra-firm tofu, pressed, cut into ¼-inch (6 mm) planks

3 cups cubed butternut squash (about 1 pound/455 g)

1 bunch broccoli rabe, ends trimmed and discarded, roughly chopped into 1-inch (2.5 cm) pieces

1 teaspoon dried oregano

½ teaspoon kosher salt

Freshly ground black pepper

¼ teaspoon crushed red pepper

1 tablespoon Calabrian chile paste (or chile paste of choice)

2 teaspoons honey

Juice of 1 lemon

2 cloves garlic, grated

This recipe goes out to everyone who loves spice. The sublime flavor and heat of Calabrian chiles (so darn elegant, they are) make a lovely match for the sweet butternut squash. If you prefer something a little less spicy, worry not, just swap the chile paste for a sweet chile sauce.

✦ Preheat the oven to 425°F (220°C). Coat a rimmed sheet pan with olive oil. Add the tofu, butternut squash, and broccoli rabe. Sprinkle the oregano, salt, black pepper, and crushed red pepper on top of the vegetables and tofu, then add 1 tablespoon of the olive oil and use your hands to evenly distribute the oil and spices.

✦ Roast for 20 minutes. While the tofu and vegetables roast, make the glaze by adding the remaining 2 tablespoons olive oil, the Calabrian chile paste, honey, lemon juice, and garlic to a small saucepan. Bring the mixture to a boil, then reduce heat to a simmer and cook for 1 to 2 minutes, or until thickened.

✦ Remove the sheet pan from the oven and brush both sides of the tofu with the glaze. Drizzle the remaining glaze all over the vegetables. Return the pan to the oven and bake for an additional 20 minutes, or until the squash and broccoli are tender.

PREP IN ADVANCE
Chop the vegetables, press and cut the tofu, prepare the glaze, and refrigerate, so that you can quickly assemble and roast the ingredients up to 24 hours later.

PREP TIME
10 minutes

COOK TIME
40 minutes

SERVES
2 to 4

Maple- and Tahini-Glazed Sheet-Pan Tofu

with SWEET POTATOES

Olive oil, for the pan

2 medium sweet potatoes, peeled and cut into wedges (about 2 pounds/910 g)

Kosher salt and freshly ground black pepper

¼ cup (60 ml) tahini

¼ cup (60 ml) maple syrup

2 tablespoons soy sauce

1 tablespoon toasted sesame oil

Juice of 1 lime

2 cloves garlic, grated

1-inch piece fresh ginger, peeled and grated

Pinch crushed red pepper

1 (14-ounce/400 g) block extra-firm tofu, pressed and cut into ¼-inch (6 mm) planks or 1-inch (2.5 cm) cubes

3 scallions, thinly sliced, for garnish

This hearty sheet-pan dinner will make a tofu lover out of even the most committeed carnivore. The tahini in the glaze adds richness and a nutty, earthy flavor, and it pairs beautifully with so many sides. I like to serve this with some cooked soba or Chinese noodles, tossing the excess glaze with the noodles and plating the tofu and sweet potatoes on top. Don't have tahini? Substitute almond, peanut, or cashew butter.

‣ Preheat the oven to 450°F (230°C). Coat a rimmed sheet pan with olive oil.

‣ Scatter the sweet potato wedges on the prepared pan and season with salt and black pepper.

‣ Make the glaze by whisking together the tahini, maple syrup, soy sauce, sesame oil, lime juice, garlic, ginger, and crushed red pepper in a medium bowl. Add half of the glaze to the pan with the sweet potatoes and toss to coat, reserving the rest.

‣ Dip the tofu planks in the reserved glaze, then add them to the pan in an even layer. Save the excess glaze for serving.

‣ Roast in the preheated oven for 40 minutes, flipping the tofu and sweet potatoes halfway through, or until the potatoes are tender and are beginning to caramelize and the tofu is golden.

‣ Remove from the oven and sprinkle with scallions before serving.

Pressing tofu before cooking with it removes much of the water tofu absorbs when it is made and packed, allowing it to really absorb the flavors of the other ingredients you are cooking with. If you have a tofu press, now is the time to use it. If you don't have one, before using tofu simply wrap it in paper towels or a clean tea towel and set it under a heavy pan, stack of books, or a few cans of food for at least 30 minutes to draw out excess moisture.

TO ENJOY LATER

The baked tofu can be cooled and then refrigerated in an airtight container for up to 3 days. To rewarm, microwave for 60 seconds, place in a preheated 250°F (120°C) oven for 6 minutes, or in an air fryer at 350°F (175°C) for 4 minutes.

PREP IN ADVANCE

Chop the vegetables, press and cut the tofu, and prepare the glaze, so that you can quickly assemble and roast later in the day.

PREP TIME
15 minutes

COOK TIME
20 minutes

SERVES
4 to 6

Middle Eastern Butternut Squash Sauté

2 tablespoons olive oil

1 teaspoon fenugreek seeds

1 small yellow onion, finely diced

½ teaspoon ground turmeric

2 tablespoons minced fresh ginger

¼ teaspoon red chili powder

1 medium butternut squash (about 2 pounds/910 g), peeled, seeded, and cut into ½-inch (12 mm) cubes

1 teaspoon kosher salt, plus more as needed

1 (28-ounce/795 g) can diced tomatoes with juice

2 tablespoons fresh lime juice (from about 1 lime), plus more as needed

2 tablespoons maple syrup

2 tablespoons chopped fresh cilantro (leaves and stems), for garnish

If I had to name the one recipe that I make most often from this book, this powerhouse of deep flavor would be the winner. It is so frustrating when vegetables spoil before we can use them, but the beauty of butternut squash is that its strong peel allows it to stay on your counter for up to two or three months, so I tend to stock up on a few. Not only are butternut squash also a good value, they're a vitamin and mineral monster, as well as the perfect canvas for all of those herbs and spices that you've been dying to use from your pantry.

✦ Heat the olive oil in a large sauté pan over low-medium heat. Add the fenugreek seeds, give them a shake, then add the onions and turmeric and sauté until the onions are soft, about 3 to 4 minutes. Add the ginger and chili powder and cook for 1 minute. Add the butternut squash and salt, cover, and cook until the squash is tender, about 10 to 12 minutes.

✦ Stir in the tomatoes, lime juice, and maple syrup. Reduce the heat to low, cover, and cook until the squash is fork tender, about 5 minutes, and then top with the cilantro. (Alternatively, after the squash is sautéed, all of the ingredients can be placed in a slow cooker over high heat for 3 to 4 hours.)

To turn this into a complete meal, serve the squash on top of cooked quinoa, rice, couscous, or other favorite grain, along with a protein, if desired.

TO ENJOY LATER
The squash can be cooled and then refrigerated in an airtight container for up to 4 days.

PREP IN ADVANCE
The vegetables and spices can be measured and chopped in the morning and cooked later in the day.

Summer Vegetables
with LEMON YOGURT–GREMOLATA DIP

PREP TIME
10 minutes

COOK TIME
25 minutes

SERVES
4

VEGETABLES
2 yellow summer squash, cut into 1-inch (2.5 cm) pieces

2 zucchini, cut into 1-inch (2.5 cm) pieces

8 spears of asparagus, woody ends removed

1 red bell pepper, cut into wedges

10 pieces fresh okra

1 red onion, cut into wedges

Nonstick cooking spray

Kosher salt and freshly ground black pepper

DIP
1 cup plain Greek yogurt

Juice of 1 small lemon plus 1 teaspoon zest

2 teaspoons dried parsley

2 cloves garlic, minced

1 teaspoon kosher salt

Freshly ground black pepper

Crispy on the outside, moist and tender inside, these vegetables say summer to me, but you can adapt this recipe to whatever veg are in season.

✦ Preheat the oven to at 400°F (205°C). Place the squash, zucchini, asparagus, bell pepper, okra, and onion in an air-fryer basket and coat them with cooking spray. Season with salt and black pepper and shake the basket to make sure the vegetables are thoroughly coated. Cook for 20 to 25 minutes or until golden outside and tender inside. *(Alternatively, the vegetables can be placed on a parchment-lined sheet pan and baked at 400°F [205°C] for 30 minutes or until golden.)*

✦ Make the dip: Place the yogurt, lemon, parsley, garlic, salt, and black pepper in a small bowl and stir to combine.

✦ Serve the golden vegetables with the dipping sauce.

During the fall and winter, you can use butternut, delicata, and/or kabocha squash, sweet potatoes, yams, onions, Brussels sprouts, Jerusalem artichokes, and parsnips instead.

TO ENJOY LATER
The vegetables and dip can be cooled and then refrigerated in separate airtight containers for up to 4 days.

PREP IN ADVANCE
The vegetables can be prepped in the morning and cooked later in the day. The dip can be made the day before serving and stored in an airtight container in the fridge.

REPURPOSE LEFTOVERS
I make twice the amount of dip and add ¼ cup (60 ml) olive oil to the extra portion to make a creamy dressing for vegetables and favorite salad greens. Double the vegetables to add alongside air fried salmon (page 155) or place on top of salad greens.

Cauliflower

with OLIVE-CAPER VINAIGRETTE

1 head medium-large cauliflower, cut into florets

2 tablespoons olive oil, divided

2 teaspoons anchovy paste, or 4 minced anchovy fillets

1 clove garlic, minced

2 tablespoons olive oil

1 tablespoon fresh lemon juice

2 tablespoons capers, drained

Pinch crushed red pepper

Freshly ground black pepper

For the first fifteen or so years of our relationship, my husband spent very little time in the kitchen. He's a really good cook, but between parenting and his work, there was little time for him to take on mealtime. During the pandemic, that all changed. Every time I turned around, he was trying out new recipes or offering to cook for us. This side dish was one of the highlights that emerged. It's so flavorful that it's often the star on the plate. Hubby says the key is the addition of anchovy paste. He's always been an anchovy lover, and a tube of paste lasts up to eighteen months in the fridge, so we always have some on hand to give dishes like this one a deep umami flavor throughout. I guarantee this becomes your new cauliflower go-to.

✦ Place the cauliflower florets in the basket of an air fryer and spritz with nonstick cooking spray. Air fry at 400°F (205°C) for 15 minutes or until golden. *(Alternatively, you can toss the florets with olive oil and roast them on a parchment-lined baking sheet at 425°F [220°C] for 25 minutes or until golden. Or the cauliflower can be steamed over boiling water for 8 minutes or until fork tender.)*

✦ While the cauliflower is cooking, to a glass jar add the anchovy paste, garlic, olive oil, lemon juice, capers, crushed red pepper, and black pepper to taste and shake until emulsified. Pour about one-half of the vinaigrette over the cauliflower, or to taste, and serve the remaining alongside for anyone who wants to drink it up, cause it's that good!

Want to keep this vegetarian or vegan? Just omit the anchovy and double up on the capers.

TO ENJOY LATER

The cooked cauliflower can be cooled and then refrigerated in an airtight container for up to 4 days.

REPURPOSE LEFTOVERS

The remaining cauliflower and vinaigrette can be added on to salad greens, into cooked pasta, or pureed and used as a dip for pita chips or as a sandwich spread.

Smashed Brussels Sprouts

PREP TIME
5 minutes

COOK TIME
25 minutes

SERVES
4 to 6

Kosher salt

1 pound (455 g) Brussels sprouts, trimmed, loose leaves discarded

3 tablespoons olive oil

Flaky salt

Freshly ground black pepper

This is truly the vegetable side dish of my dreams; the sprouts remain tender and soft on the inside but develop beautiful crispy edges thanks to the time spent finishing in the oven.

◆ Preheat the oven to 425°F (220°C). Bring a medium pot of salted water to a boil. Once boiling, add the Brussels sprouts and cook for 5 minutes, or until fork tender. Remove from heat and drain, then pat dry with a clean tea towel or paper towel.

◆ Add 1½ tablespoons olive oil to a rimmed sheet pan and use a pastry brush or paper towel to spread into an even layer, ensuring the entire surface is coated.

◆ Add the Brussels sprouts, then smash each sprout with the bottom of a mug or glass. Brush the smashed Brussels sprouts with the remaining 1½ tablespoons olive oil, then season with flaky salt and black pepper.

◆ Roast in the preheated oven for 10 minutes, then flip the sprouts over and roast them for an additional 10 minutes, or until golden and crisp. *(Alternatively, take the boiled and smashed sprouts and pop them in an air fryer at 375°F [190°C] for 10 minutes, flipping halfway through cooking time.)*

When picking Brussels sprouts I like to grab large ones that have more leaves, which will get crispy when roasted or air fried.

TO ENJOY LATER
The Brussels sprouts can be cooled and refrigerated in an airtight container for up to 4 days. To reheat, place in air fryer at 400°F (205°C) for 5 minutes or in a preheated 350°F (175°C) oven for 10 minutes.

REPURPOSE LEFTOVERS
Smashed Brussels sprouts can be added to favorite salads or vegetarian sandwiches.

Smashed Potatoes

with CRISPY CAPERS

PREP TIME
5 minutes

COOK TIME
50 minutes

SERVES
4

Nonstick olive-oil
cooking spray

1½ pounds (680 g) baby
potatoes, scrubbed

Kosher salt and freshly
ground black pepper

2 tablespoons capers,
patted dry

2 tablespoons freshly
grated Parmesan
cheese

2 tablespoons
chopped fresh flat- or
curly-leaf parsley

Juice of ½ lemon

These smashed potatoes hold a very special place in my heart. They possess all of the best qualities a good potato recipe should have—a crisp french fry–like exterior with a creamy mashed potato–like interior. Throw in a few crisp, salty capers and you have the ultimate crowd-pleasing side dish.

+ Preheat the oven to 450°F (230°C) and spray a large rimmed sheet pan with olive oil cooking spray.

+ Add the potatoes to a medium pot and cover with cold water by 1 inch (2.5 cm). Generously season the water with kosher salt, then bring to a boil over medium-high heat. Once the water reaches a boil, cook the potatoes for 10 minutes, or until they are fork tender. Remove from the heat and drain.

+ Place the potatoes on the prepared sheet pan, and using the bottom of a heavy glass or jar, smash the potatoes flat. Spray the tops with more olive oil, and season with salt and pepper. *(Alternatively, the baby potatoes can be air fried at 400°F [205°C] for 18 minutes or until tender inside and golden outside. Add the capers to the air fryer and cook for an additional 3 to 4 minutes or until the capers are crispy.)*

+ If baking in the oven, scatter the capers over the potatoes and bake on the sheet pan for 10 minutes. Flip the potatoes over and bake for 15 more minutes. Remove from the oven and sprinkle with the Parmesan cheese and parsley, then return to the oven for 2 more minutes, or until the cheese is melted and starts to crisp.

+ Transfer the potato and caper mixture to a serving tray, drizzle the lemon juice on top, and serve immediately.

Make sure to really dry your capers when you take them out of the brine, which will ensure they get nice and crisp in the oven!

TO ENJOY LATER
The potatoes can be cooled and refrigerated in an airtight container for up to 4 days. To reheat, place in air fryer at 400°F (205°C) for 5 minutes or in a preheated 350°F (175°C) oven for 10 minutes.

REPURPOSE LEFTOVERS
Smashed potatoes can be added to Quesadillas (page 227), Any Veggie Frittata (page 60), or vegetarian sandwiches.

124 Refrigerator

PREP TIME
5 minutes

COOK TIME
n/a

MAKES
½ cup (120 ml)

Everyday Vinaigrette, Five Ways

6 tablespoons (90 ml) olive oil

¼ cup (60 ml) fresh lemon juice (about 1½ lemons)

1 teaspoon sugar or honey

Pinch kosher salt

Freshly ground black pepper

My very favorite restaurant in Los Angeles is the sublime All-Time. Their Good Ass Salad is a beautifully balanced combination of market-fresh greens, fruit, and seasonal vegetables. It's topped with their luscious, zippy dressing, a subtle burst of lemony deliciousness that always delights my taste buds. The simplicity of it is what I most admire—it makes itself known while allowing the flavor of every ingredient to shine through. While I dare not attempt to obtain the recipe from All-Time's divine owners, Ashley and Tyler, I've done my best (after countless times eating theirs) to recreate it here. You can also use this recipe as a base and adapt it into endless combinations. I've included four variations of my own below.

Place all of the ingredients in a jar and shake vigorously. Taste and adjust seasoning, as needed. Store in the refrigerator for up to 2 weeks.

VARIATIONS

1. **Lemon Dijon Vinaigrette:** Place the Everyday Vinaigrette ingredients, 2 teaspoons Dijon mustard, and 1 small chopped shallot into a blender or food processor and puree until smooth. Taste and adjust seasoning, as needed.

2. **Citrus Cilantro Vinaigrette:** Place the Everyday Vinaigrette ingredients, ¼ cup (7.5 g) loosely packed fresh cilantro (leaves and stems), 1 small chopped shallot, and 1 clove garlic into a blender or food processor and puree until smooth. Taste and adjust seasoning, as needed.

3. **Creamy Feta Vinaigrette:** Place the Everyday Vinaigrette ingredients and 2 tablespoons feta cheese into a blender or food processor and puree until smooth. Taste and adjust seasoning, as needed.

4. **Basil Vinaigrette:** Place the Everyday Vinaigrette ingredients, ¼ cup (7.5 g) fresh basil (leaves and stems), 1 small chopped shallot, and 1 clove garlic into a blender or food processor and puree until smooth. Taste and adjust seasoning, as needed.

This vinaigrette is all about the ingredients you use to make it. So, invest in a really good bottle of olive oil and use fresh lemon. Go wild and try making it with a pink or Meyer lemon if you can get your hands on one. Don't want to use sugar? Honey makes the perfect substitute.

REPURPOSE LEFTOVERS
All of these vinaigrettes can be tossed with favorite grains, greens and vegetables, nuts, seeds, and proteins to make cold salads.

PREP TIME
5 minutes

COOK TIME
n/a

MAKES
⅔ cup (165 ml)

Creamy Balsamic Vinaigrette

¼ cup (120 ml) mayonnaise

3 tablespoons balsamic vinegar

3 tablespoons olive oil

2 teaspoons Dijon mustard

½ teaspoon garlic powder

Pinch kosher salt

Freshly ground black pepper

Not sure what to make in a pinch? Keep a homemade balsamic dressing on hand in your fridge, and you'll have at least five recipes ready to go in a matter of minutes. This Creamy Balsamic Vinaigrette is a workhorse. Whether you're using it to marinate the chicken you're going to roast or grill, drizzling it on top of perfectly caramelized roast vegetables, serving it as a dip for crudité, or tossing it with arugula or other fresh greens, the zip, zing, and tang of this recipe will liven up anything you partner it with.

Place the ingredients in a bowl and, using a small whisk or fork, combine until creamy. *(Alternatively, you can place the ingredients in a jar and shake vigorously until emulsified.)* Use immediately or refrigerate for up to 2 weeks.

While a traditional balsamic vinegar is what I most often use, substituting white balsamic or sherry vinegar gives this dressing an added dimension. Don't have mayonnaise? Try full-fat or low-fat Greek yogurt to provide the creaminess (and an extra hit of protein to boot).

REPURPOSE LEFTOVERS
Use vinaigrette to marinade chicken for several hours before grilling, air frying, or roasting.

PREP TIME
10 minutes

COOK TIME
n/a

MAKES
1½ cups (360 ml)

Green Goddess Dressing

1 cup (240 ml) plain Greek yogurt

2 tablespoons fresh lemon juice

⅓ cup (75 ml) olive oil

1 cup (50 g) chopped fresh flat- or curly-leaf parsley (leaves and stems)

1 cup (30 g) loosely packed fresh herbs *(dill, cilantro, chervil, chives, mint, tarragon, basil, and/or fresh spinach)*

1 anchovy fillet, 2 teaspoons anchovy paste, or 2 teaspoons capers

½ teaspoon garlic powder

Pinch kosher salt

Freshly ground black pepper

This recipe is reason number 37,564 homemade dressings are worth the few minutes it takes to prepare them. Fresh herbs make for a flavor-packed treat that's hard to replicate in a shelf-stable bottled dressing. This dressing should not be limited to use with salads; it's so much more versatile. Use it as a dip for chips or raw vegetables like cucumbers, radishes, or avocado slices; as a topper for broiled fish; and so much more. Substituting capers for the anchovies maintains this dressing's fantastic umami hit while making it perfect for vegans and vegetarians alike.

Place the ingredients in a food processor or blender and puree until smooth. Use immediately or place in a jar or bottle and refrigerate for up to 1 week.

Don't have Greek yogurt? Sour cream and/or mayonnaise are ideal substitutes.

PREP TIME
10 minutes

COOK TIME
n/a

MAKES
1 cup

Any Green Pesto

5 cups (about 150 g) packed greens or herbs of choice, such as basil, baby arugula, baby spinach, or shredded kale

½ cup (50 g) grated Parmesan cheese

¼ cup (35 g) pine nuts

Juice of 1 lemon

1 clove garlic, grated

½ cup (120 ml) olive oil

Kosher salt and freshly ground black pepper

Crushed red pepper (optional)

Got some herbs or greens in the fridge that are looking a little lackluster? Consider that your sign to make a batch of this versatile pesto. You can keep it classic by using all fresh basil, or get creative by adding in some baby arugula or spinach, or chopped kale.

In a high-speed blender or food processor, add the greens, cheese, pine nuts, lemon juice, garlic, olive oil, salt, black pepper, and crushed red pepper, if using. Process until smooth, then taste and adjust seasoning as needed.

Pesto has so many uses! Store it in the fridge to toss with pasta, slather it on sandwiches, or use it as a dip. Freeze cubes of it to add bursts of flavor to vinaigrettes, scrambled eggs, soups, and more.

TO ENJOY LATER
Place the pesto in an airtight container, then drizzle a thin layer of olive oil on top. This will ensure the pesto stays vibrant and green for up to 3 days when tightly sealed. To store for longer use, divide the pesto into ice cube trays and freeze until solid. Once frozen, remove the cubes from the tray and store in a freezer-safe container for up to 3 months.

REPURPOSE LEFTOVERS
Pesto can be tossed with cooked pasta, grains, and chicken, or used as a pizza topping.

PREP TIME
10 minutes

COOK TIME
n/a

MAKES
8 tablespoons
(1 stick/225 g)

Compound Butter, Three Ways

8 tablespoons
(1 stick/225 g) unsalted
butter, softened to
room temperature

**1. MIX-INS FOR
CINNAMON-SUGAR
COMPOUND BUTTER**
2 tablespoons sugar

1 tablespoon ground
cinnamon

**2. MIX-INS FOR
LEMON-HERB
COMPOUND BUTTER**
2 tablespoons
chopped fresh flat- or
curly-leaf parsley, dill,
cilantro, chives, or a
mix

Zest of 1 lemon

**3. MIX-INS FOR
CHEESY COMPOUND
BUTTER**
2 tablespoons grated
Parmesan cheese

1½ teaspoons freshly
ground black pepper

Can you improve butter? Seems like a tough one, but how about cinnamon-sugar butter? Or lemon-herb butter? Or Parm-infused butter?! The butter is your blank canvas, so feel free to get creative with the mix-ins.

✦ Add the butter to a medium bowl. Mash with the back of a fork. In a separate small bowl, stir together the mix-ins, then scatter on top of the softened butter. Using a spatula, gently fold the mix-ins into the butter until evenly blended.

✦ Place an 8 by 11-inch (20 by 28 cm) rectangle of parchment on your work surface, then scrape the butter mixture into the middle. Using your hand and the spatula, scrape it into a rough cylinder. Using the parchment as a wrapper, roll the butter into a cylinder, shaping as you roll. Place the cylinder on a sheet of plastic wrap, then twist into a tight cylinder. Set in the fridge to chill until firm, about 4 hours.

I keep a variety of parchment-wrapped rolls of these flavor-rich butters on hand at all times. Use these butters to brighten pasta and rice, or to turn a slice of ordinary toasted bread into something exquisite. Compound butters can also add an extra hit of flavor to popcorn, a grilled cheese sandwich, and mashed potatoes, or put a pat on top of cooked meat and seafood for added richness.

TO ENJOY LATER
Store the butter in plastic-wrapped rolls of parchment paper in the fridge for up to 6 days, or in the freezer for up to 6 months.

Cauliflower Fried Rice

2 tablespoons olive oil or butter

2 large eggs, whisked

1 teaspoon kosher salt

1 small yellow onion, diced

1 large carrot, diced

2 cloves garlic, chopped

2 teaspoons fresh ginger, minced

1 head cauliflower, chopped in food processor until the pieces resemble rice, or 1 (10- to 12-ounce/280- to 340 g) bag frozen cauliflower rice

1 cup (145 g) fresh or frozen peas

3 scallions, diced (green and white parts)

2 teaspoons sesame oil

3 tablespoons low-sodium soy sauce

2 tablespoons toasted sesame seeds (optional)

I love a one-pot meal, especially when it's chock full of vegetables like this one. You won't miss the meat at all in this intensely flavorful fried rice that will resemble your childhood favorite, only it's a whole lot lighter.

+ Heat 1 tablespoon of the olive oil in a large sauté pan or wok over medium heat. Pour in the eggs, sprinkle them with ½ teaspoon salt, and cook for 1 minute or until just scrambled. Remove to a plate.

+ Return the pan to medium heat, add the remaining 1 tablespoon oil, and sauté the onion and carrots for 4 minutes or until almost fork tender. Add the garlic, ginger, cauliflower, and remaining ½ teaspoon salt and sauté for an additional 3 to 4 minutes, or until cauliflower is fork tender. Add the peas, scallions, sesame oil, soy sauce, and scrambled egg, and cook an additional minute, or until vegetables are tender and everything is thoroughly warmed through. Sprinkle with sesame seeds, if using, for an extra hit of protein.

This is the recipe to utilize any vegetable you may have lying around, whether that is bell peppers, edamame, celery, zucchini, butternut squash, broccoli, fresh spinach, or corn. Simply chop them into bite-size pieces and sauté them with the onions and carrots until just fork tender. Want to jazz it up even more? Add your favorite canned beans, rinsed and drained, or add sautéed shrimp, scallops, chopped skirt or hanger steak, or rotisserie chicken.

TO ENJOY LATER
The cooked rice can be cooled and then refrigerated in an airtight container for up to 4 days. To rewarm, microwave for 60 seconds or eat at room temperature.

REPURPOSE LEFTOVERS
Place the cauliflower rice over your favorite grain and warm through or eat at room temperature.

Crispy Artichoke Hearts

with CAESAR DIP

ARTICHOKE HEARTS
1 (12-ounce/340 g)
bag frozen quartered
artichoke hearts, or 2
cans (14-ounce/400 g)
water-packed
quartered artichoke
hearts, drained

Nonstick olive-oil
cooking spray

½ teaspoon garlic
powder

½ teaspoon onion
powder

½ teaspoon paprika

½ teaspoon kosher salt

DIP
5 tablespoons (30 g)
Parmesan cheese

2 tablespoons fresh
lemon juice

2 large egg yolks

1 clove garlic

1 teaspoon Dijon
mustard

4 anchovy fillets, or 1
tablespoon anchovy
paste

3 tablespoons olive oil

My family is utterly addicted to these air-fried artichokes. Every time I make them, they disappear within minutes. Not only are they super light and healthy, but they satisfy that craving for something briny, crispy, and savory all at once. These are best when made in the air fryer, but are still tasty if roasted in the oven.

◆ Place the artichoke hearts in an air-fryer basket. Using olive oil spray, thoroughly coat the artichoke hearts. Sprinkle them all over with the garlic powder, onion powder, paprika, and salt. Cook on 400°F (205°C) for 14 to 16 minutes, or until the artichoke leaves start to turn golden and the edges of the leaves start to crisp. *(Alternatively, preheat the oven to 425°F [220°C] and bake the artichokes on a parchment-lined baking sheet for 25 minutes, or until the leaves are golden and crispy.)*

◆ While the artichoke hearts are cooking, make the Caesar dip. Place 3 tablespoons of the Parmesan, the lemon juice, egg yolks, garlic, mustard, anchovies, and olive oil in a food processor or blender. Puree until smooth and creamy.

◆ After the artichoke hearts finish cooking, remove them to a platter and sprinkle with the remaining 2 tablespoons Parmesan cheese. Serve with the dip.

If you can only find whole artichoke hearts, just drain them and cut them into quarters. You can substitute olive oil–packed artichoke hearts, but make sure to blot them well first with a towel to remove excess oil.

REPURPOSE LEFTOVERS
Serve any leftover raw or cooked vegetables and grilled chicken or fish with the Caesar dip.

Lentil Pot Pie

PREP TIME
20 minutes

COOK TIME
60 minutes

SERVES
4 to 6

1 tablespoon olive oil, plus more for brushing

1 onion, diced

1 teaspoon dried thyme

1 teaspoon dried parsley

Kosher salt and freshly ground black pepper

1 tablespoon tomato paste

⅓ cup (75 ml) white wine

1 cup (200 g) red lentils, rinsed

4 cups (32-ounce/960 ml) vegetable stock

2 medium sweet potatoes (about 8 ounces/225 g), peeled and diced

1 (10-ounce/280 g) bag frozen mixed vegetables

All-purpose flour, for rolling pastry

1 sheet store-bought puff pastry, thawed if frozen

1 large egg

Lentils are high in fiber and cook fast, making this a healthy and easy spin on the classic chicken pot pie.

◆ Preheat the oven to 425°F (220°C).

◆ Heat the olive oil in a deep 10-inch (25 cm) oven-safe frying pan over medium heat. Once shimmering, add the onion, thyme, and parsley and cook for 5 minutes, or until the onion is soft and golden.

◆ Season with salt and pepper, then add the tomato paste, stirring to evenly coat the onions. Cook for 1 to 2 minutes, then pour in the wine to deglaze, scraping up any brown bits that have formed on the bottom of the pan. Cook for 1 minute, or until the wine has reduced by half. Add the lentils and 3 cups (720 ml) of the vegetable stock and bring to a boil.

◆ Add the sweet potatoes and reduce to a simmer. Cook over low heat for 15 minutes, or until the lentils and sweet potatoes are tender. Turn off the heat and stir in the remaining 1 cup (240 ml) vegetable stock and the frozen veggies. Set aside.

◆ On a lightly floured surface, use a rolling pin to smooth out the seams in the puff pastry. Drape the pastry sheet over the frying pan, trimming the edges with kitchen shears. Whisk the egg with a pinch of salt to make a wash. Cut a few vents in the center of the pastry, brush with the egg wash, then bake for 30 to 35 minutes, or until the crust is flaky and golden.

This recipe is versatile. Cooking for carnivores? Add in some chopped rotisserie chicken. To keep this vegan, use vegan puff pastry and skip the egg wash in the recipe.

TO ENJOY LATER

After baking, the pie can be cooled, covered in foil or plastic wrap, and refrigerated for up to 3 days. To rewarm, microwave servings for 60 seconds or place frying pan in a preheated 300°F (150°C) oven for 12 minutes or until heated through.

PREP IN ADVANCE

The pie can be assembled as directed, covered, and refrigerated for up to 3 days. Or the assembled pie can be covered in plastic wrap, then foil, and labeled with tape using a marker. Freeze for up to 4 months. Bake as directed, adding 5 to 10 minutes to the cooking time.

Mango Morning Glory Muffins

Nonstick cooking spray

1¾ cups (220 g) whole wheat flour

¼ cup (30 g) wheat germ

½ tablespoon ground cinnamon

1 teaspoon baking powder

½ teaspoon ground ginger

½ teaspoon kosher salt

¼ teaspoon baking soda

¼ teaspoon ground nutmeg

1 cup (125 g) frozen mango chunks

½ cup (120 ml) whole milk

1 cup (200 g) sugar

2 large eggs

¾ cup (180 ml) olive oil

1 teaspoon vanilla extract

1½ cups (125 g) finely grated carrots (from about 3 large carrots)

½ cup (45 g) unsweetened shredded coconut

½ cup (75 g) raisins

Mornings are hard. A muffin can make things just a little bit easier, and I think you deserve one. These heavenly muffins are packed with vibrant mango, earthy carrots, nummy coconut, and warming spices like cinnamon, ginger, and turmeric, and they have a moist crumb thanks to the mango and olive oil.

✦ Preheat the oven to 350°F (175°C) and line a 12-cup muffin tin with paper liners, then spray the liners with nonstick spray.

✦ In a medium bowl, add the flour, wheat germ, cinnamon, baking powder, ginger, salt, baking soda, and nutmeg. Whisk to combine, then set aside.

✦ Add the mango and milk to a high-speed blender. Process until smooth, then scrape into a large bowl. Add the sugar, eggs, olive oil, and vanilla extract to the mango puree. Whisk for 2 minutes, or until very well blended.

✦ Add the dry ingredients to the wet ingredients and use a rubber spatula to fold them together until no streaks of flour remain. Fold in the carrots, coconut, and raisins until evenly distributed.

✦ Divide the batter evenly among the prepared muffin cups. Bake in the preheated oven for 30 minutes, or until a toothpick inserted in the center comes out clean. Allow muffins to cool for 10 minutes.

Mango adds a lovely tropical vibe to the muffins, but you could swap it for whatever frozen fruit you have on hand.

TO ENJOY LATER

The baked muffins can be cooled, then tightly wrapped in plastic and refrigerated for up to 3 days. To freeze, place the cooled, baked muffins in labeled zip-top bags for up to 4 months. To rewarm, microwave for 30 seconds, or place in a preheated 250°F (120°C) oven for 5 minutes or in a 350°F (175°C) air fryer for 2 minutes.

PREP IN ADVANCE

The dry ingredients can be whisked and covered on a counter. The wet ingredients can be stirred and refrigerated overnight or until ready to bake.

Smoothie Ice Pops

PREP TIME
5 minutes

COOK TIME
4 hours to overnight

MAKES
4 to 6 ice pops

---

1 large banana, peeled

¼ cup (60 ml) yogurt of choice

1 serving protein powder of choice

1 cup (240 ml) milk of choice

1 cup (about 145 to 155 g) fresh or frozen fruit of choice *(acai, blueberries, blackberries, dragon fruit, figs, kiwi, mango, papaya, peaches, pineapple, raspberries, strawberries)*

Optional flavorful add-ins: 2 tablespoons peanut, almond, or sun butter; 2 tablespoons cacao powder; 1 tablespoon matcha powder; ½ avocado, pitted and peeled; ½ cup (120 ml) pumpkin puree; 1 teaspoon chai spices, ground cinnamon, or pumpkin pie spice

It's no secret that I make smoothies almost every morning for family breakfast. On the occasions that I make too much, instead of drinking more than my belly can handle or, worse, dumping what's leftover, I pull out the popsicle molds to fill up and freeze so we can always have a nutritious snack or dessert at the ready. Especially on hot days, these Smoothie Ice Pops fly out of the freezer.

+ Place all of the ingredients in a blender and puree until smooth. Divide the mixture among 4 to 6 popsicle molds, depending on their size.

+ Freeze the ice pops for at least 4 hours and preferably overnight. Run the molds under water to loosen and remove the pops.

Want to get even more nutrition into your Smoothie Ice Pops? Add a serving of collagen peptides, 1 tablespoon of hemp or chia seeds, a teaspoon of bee pollen, and/or flax seeds.

Any Fruit Crisp

PREP TIME
15 minutes

COOK TIME
35 minutes if using
fresh fruit, 60 minutes if
using frozen fruit

SERVES
8 to 10

FILLING

8 cups (about 1¼
pounds/570 g) fruit of
choice (*mixed berries,
cherries, apples, and/
or pears*), cut into
½-inch (12 mm) pieces

Juice of 1 lemon

½ cup (100 g)
granulated sugar

¼ cup (30 g) cornstarch

1 teaspoon vanilla
extract

½ teaspoon ground
ginger

½ teaspoon ground
cinnamon

½ teaspoon kosher salt

TOPPING

½ cup (65 g) all-
purpose flour

½ cup (110 g) packed
brown sugar

½ cup (45 g) rolled oats

1 teaspoon ground
cinnamon

Pinch kosher salt

½ cup (1 stick/115 g)
cold unsalted butter,
cubed, plus more for
the pan

Vanilla ice cream or
whipped cream, for
serving

The rules of this recipe are designed to be broken. Get creative by using seasonal fruit and flavorings or ones that speak to you. Um, chopped pineapple and a little rum sprinkled with this crisp topping? Yes, please!

+ Preheat the oven to 375°F (190°C) and grease an 8-inch (20 cm) square baking dish or 10-inch (25 cm) skillet.

+ Make the filling: Place the fruit in a large bowl. Add the lemon juice, granulated sugar, cornstarch, vanilla, ginger, cinnamon, and salt and toss until well-combined. Scrape the filling into the prepared pan.

+ Set aside to make the topping: In a medium bowl, combine the flour, brown sugar, oats, cinnamon, and salt. Stir until well combined. Add the cold butter and use your fingers to work the cubes into the dry ingredients, until the butter is broken down into pea-size chunks and the mixture holds together when squeezed between your fingertips.

+ Cover the fruit filling with the crisp topping. Bake for 30 to 35 minutes if using fresh fruit, or 55 to 60 minutes if using frozen fruit, or until the fruit juices are bubbling and start to thicken and the crisp topping is golden.

+ Serve the crisp warm with a scoop of ice cream or a dollop of whipped cream.

A crisp differs from a crumble in that crisp toppings include rolled oats and a crumble topping is solely flour based. Also, no one will judge you if you eat leftovers for breakfast.

TO ENJOY LATER
The baked crisp can be cooled and refrigerated in an airtight container for up to 3 days. To rewarm, microwave for 30 seconds or place in a preheated 250°F (120°C) oven for 8 to 10 minutes.

PREP IN ADVANCE
The crisp can be assembled, covered, and then refrigerated overnight. Bake as directed.

Blueberry-Cornmeal Breakfast Cake

PREP TIME
15 minutes

COOK TIME
40 minutes

MAKES
1 (8-inch/20 cm square)
cake; 9 to 12 servings

1 cup (125 g) all-purpose flour

1 cup (165 g) fine cornmeal

2 teaspoons baking powder

1 teaspoon ground cinnamon

1 teaspoon kosher salt

½ cup (120 ml) whole milk

½ cup (120 ml) sour cream

½ cup (1 stick/115 g) unsalted butter, at room temperature

¾ cup (150 g) granulated sugar, plus 1 tablespoon for sprinkling

1 large egg, at room temperature

1 teaspoon vanilla extract

1 cup (155 g) frozen blueberries

This sumptuous cake has a moist crumb and just the right amount of sweetness to make it breakfast worthy. The addition of cornmeal adds a lovely, almost nutty flavor. I relish the little bursts of tartness the blueberries provide but any frozen berry will work.

+ Preheat the oven to 350°F (175°C) and line an 8-inch (20 cm) square baking pan with parchment paper.

+ In a medium bowl, sift together the flour, cornmeal, baking powder, cinnamon, and salt, then whisk to combine.

+ In a separate small bowl, mix together the milk and sour cream.

+ In the bowl of a standing mixer fitted with the paddle attachment, cream the butter and sugar at medium speed for 3 to 4 minutes, or until light and fluffy. Scrape down the sides of the bowl and add the egg and vanilla. Beat at medium speed for 1 minute, or until fully combined.

+ Add half of the flour mixture and mix at low speed for 30 seconds. Add all of the milk and sour cream mixture and mix at medium speed until absorbed, 1 to 2 minutes. Add the remaining flour mixture and mix at a low speed, just until no streaks of flour remain.

+ Scrape the dough into the prepared pan, smoothing it into an even layer. Top with frozen blueberries, spreading them into an even layer. Sprinkle the top with 1 tablespoon granulated sugar and bake for 40 minutes, or until a toothpick inserted in the center comes out clean.

Feel free to play with the spices. Cinnamon and blueberries are a classic combination, but a touch of ground cardamom and ginger are lovely!

Gluten free? Swap the all-purpose flour for your favorite gluten-free all-purpose flour (I love Cup4Cup).

TO ENJOY LATER

After baking, let the cake cool, wrap in plastic, and refrigerate for up to 3 days. To freeze, cut the cooled cake into slices and place into labeled zip-top bags. To rewarm, microwave for 30 seconds, place in a preheated 250°F (120°C) oven for 5 minutes, or in an air fryer at 350°F (175°C) for 2 minutes.

PREP IN ADVANCE

The dry ingredients can be whisked and stored covered. The wet ingredients can be stirred and refrigerated for up to 2 days.

Zippy Fish Tacos

PREP TIME
15 minutes

COOK TIME
20 minutes

SERVES
4

½ small red onion, thinly sliced

½ cup (120 ml) white vinegar

1 tablespoon sugar

2½ teaspoons kosher salt

1 small head cabbage, shredded

3 tablespoons olive oil

2 tablespoons fresh lime juice *(about 1 lime)*

1 avocado, pitted and peeled

¼ cup (60 ml) sour cream

2 tablespoons finely chopped fresh cilantro (leaves and stems)

1 pound (455 g) whitefish

1 teaspoon paprika

1 teaspoon ground cumin

½ teaspoon garlic powder

12 flour or corn tortillas

1 tomato, diced

Pickled jalapeños

I love fish prepared many ways—meunière, sashimi, southern fried, ceviche, and more—but simple sautéed fish tacos are still my preferred way to use whitefish (e.g., sole, halibut, cod, snapper, or grouper). Served in warm tortillas and topped with crunchy slaw, pickled onion, and a citrus avocado sauce, they are a total comfort food.

✦ Add the onion, vinegar, ½ cup (120 ml) water, the sugar, and 1 teaspoon salt in a small saucepan. Bring to a boil, reduce to a simmer, and stir to combine. Let sit for 10 minutes to cool.

✦ In a medium bowl, add the shredded cabbage, ½ teaspoon salt, 1 tablespoon of the olive oil, and 1 tablespoon lime juice and toss to combine.

✦ Place the avocado and ½ teaspoon salt in a medium bowl and mash together. Add the sour cream, cilantro, and the remaining lime juice, and stir to combine.

✦ Place the fish on a plate and sprinkle with paprika, cumin, garlic powder, and ½ teaspoon salt. Heat a large sauté pan over medium-high heat, and add the remaining 2 tablespoons olive oil. When hot, add the fish fillets and sauté on each side for 2 to 3 minutes. Remove to a clean plate. *(Alternatively, the fish can be coated with cooking spray and air fried at 400°F [205°C] for 4 to 5 minutes, or until golden and cooked through.)*

✦ Place the tortillas over a gas flame for 1 minute on each side to warm through. *(Alternatively, you can air fry or microwave the tortillas for 1 minute.)*

✦ Place the tortillas on plates and top with the cabbage mixture, sautéed fish, avocado cream, pickled onions, then finish with the diced tomato and pickled jalapeños.

If using defrosted whitefish, make sure to blot the fillets well with a paper or hand towel to remove as much water as possible. This will help to make the fish even crispier when cooked.

TO ENJOY LATER
The cooked fish and the prepared taco fillings can be cooled and refrigerated in airtight containers for up to 24 hours.

PREP IN ADVANCE
The cabbage can be prepared up to 24 hours ahead and the pickled onions up to 2 weeks ahead. Store in airtight containers in the fridge.

Shrimp and Artichoke Fra Diavolo

PREP TIME
10 minutes

COOK TIME
12 minutes

SERVES
4

1 pound (455 g) medium or large frozen shrimp, defrosted, peeled, and deveined

4 tablespoons olive oil

1 teaspoon crushed red pepper (*less if you don't like your food spicy and more if you want more intense heat*)

1 teaspoon kosher salt, plus more as needed

8 cloves garlic, minced

1 cup (240 ml) white wine

1 (28-ounce/795 g) can diced tomatoes, drained

1 teaspoon sugar

1 (12-ounce/340 g) bag frozen artichoke hearts, or 1 can (14-ounce/400 g) quartered artichoke hearts, drained

1 pound (455 g) linguine or spaghetti

Freshly ground black pepper (optional)

Sure, going out for dinner to an upscale Italian restaurant can be fun, delicious, even romantic, but I'd proffer that using your pantry staples to make the exact same meal at home is just as fun, delicious, and, yes, romantic, if not more so. I always have the ingredients for this recipe in my kitchen because of how adaptable they are and also because when combined, they make one of those "You made this?!," enviable meals your friends will salivate over. Garlicky, spicy shrimp tossed with artichoke hearts and linguine or spaghetti results in the most satisfying dish you can imagine. And you don't have to get all dressed up to have it.

+ Place the shrimp, 2 tablespoons of the olive oil, and the crushed red pepper in a medium bowl and toss to coat.

+ Bring a large pot of salted water to a boil.

+ Heat a large sauté pan over medium heat, add the shrimp in one layer, and sauté for 2 minutes. Flip the shrimp and cook until the shrimp are pink throughout, about 1 minute more. Transfer to a bowl.

+ Place the large sauté pan over medium heat, add the remaining 2 tablespoons olive oil, and sauté the garlic over low to medium heat for 1 minute. Pour in the wine and simmer for 2 minutes. Add the tomatoes, sugar, 1 teaspoon salt, and artichokes and stir to combine. Raise the heat to medium-high and simmer the sauce for 5 minutes, or until it starts to reduce.

+ While the sauce is simmering, cook the pasta according to package directions, reserving ½ cup (120 ml) of the pasta liquid.

+ Place the pasta and shrimp into the sauce and stir to coat over low heat for 1 minute. Add the reserved pasta water if the sauce is too thick, and season with salt and black pepper, if desired.

To defrost frozen shrimp, place the shrimp in the refrigerator overnight or cover with room-temperature water and allow to sit out until defrosted, about 10 minutes, changing the water when it becomes too cold.

For even more depth of flavor, add 1 teaspoon dried basil or Italian herbs while making the tomato sauce, or fresh basil or parsley to finish the dish.

TO ENJOY LATER
The Fra Diavolo can be cooled and then refrigerated in an airtight container for up to 24 hours.

Salmon

with LEMON-HERB BUTTER

PREP TIME
5 minutes

COOK TIME
15 minutes

SERVES
3 to 4

1 pound (455 g) frozen salmon, with or without skin, defrosted

2 teaspoons olive oil

½ teaspoon garlic powder

½ teaspoon kosher salt

1 lemon, halved

Lemon-Herb Compound Butter (page 135)

I love cooking, but I've never enjoyed doing dishes. That informs the recipes I choose to make, probably more than anything else, particularly on those nights when I can barely summon the brain power to think about what to make but know it has to be healthy and flavorful. Salmon is packed with omega-3 fatty acids and can have so much flavor. Cooked to perfection in the hassle-free air fryer, the salmon gets sumptuously golden, as does the lemon cooking alongside it. Squeezing its juices on top of the salmon after the lemon caramelizes adds a flavor profile you may only have experienced at the hands of a professional chef. Serving it with a big pat of herby compound butter that you have waiting in the fridge will leave you with a dinner that no one will believe is as simple as it gets. If you have fresh cauliflower, broccoli, zucchini, or squash on hand, simply cut them into florets or 1-inch (2.5 cm) pieces, toss with 1 teaspoon oil, or use a cooking oil spray to coat, and air fry them alongside the salmon for a complete meal.

+ Place the salmon skin side down inside the air-fryer basket. Drizzle with 1 teaspoon of the oil and sprinkle with the garlic powder and salt. Rub the lemon halves with the remaining teaspoon of oil and place them next to the salmon in the air-fryer basket.

+ Turn the air fryer to 400°F (205°C) and cook the salmon for 13 to 15 minutes or until golden. Serve with the butter. *(Alternatively, the salmon can be broiled for 10 minutes or until golden, or baked in an oven preheated to 400°F [205°C] for 12 to 13 minutes for medium rare and 14 to 15 minutes for medium.)*

+ If you can only get your hands on 4-ounce (115 g) salmon fillets, cook them for 2 minutes less with all cooking methods.

This is another recipe that welcomes you to play with your spice drawer. While I love garlic powder on my salmon, paprika, curry, onion powder, berbere (a spice mix containing chile peppers, coriander, garlic, ginger, and Ethiopian holy basil), dill, or other dried herbs can give this salmon dish an extra boost of flavor.

TO ENJOY LATER
After cooking, the salmon can be cooled and then refrigerated in an airtight container for up to 2 days. Chop to place on top of salads or in rice bowls.

REPURPOSE LEFTOVERS
Remaining salmon can be added to salad or flaked on top of warm rice with a pat of Lemon Herb Compound Butter (page 135).

Coconut Shrimp

1 pound (455 g) medium or large frozen shrimp, defrosted, peeled, and deveined

½ cup (65 g) all-purpose flour

½ teaspoon kosher salt

2 large eggs

1 cup (85 g) shredded unsweetened coconut

Nonstick cooking spray, if air frying or baking

Olive, canola, avocado, or vegetable oil, if sauteing

On a childhood family vacation in Hawaii, I had my first coconut shrimp. It was bite-size, slightly sweet, and crunchy! And while I love a homemade sauce as much as the next girl, this is the time to rely on your favorite store-bought one from the fridge door and spend your time making the crispy, crunchy beauties. (Though, who knows, maybe you've already made my Creamy Balsamic Vinaigrette, page 128, or Green Goddess Dressing, page 131, and will get to go full homemade after all!) Serve them as an appetizer to friends or share with a loved one as an entree.

✦ Place the shrimp on a clean towel or paper towels to thoroughly blot dry.

✦ Create an assembly line with 3 medium to large shallow bowls. Place the flour and salt in the first bowl and whisk to combine. Crack the eggs into the second bowl and whisk to combine. Place the coconut in the third bowl.

✦ Add the shrimp to the flour bowl, toss to coat all over, and tap excess flour off each shrimp. Dunk the shrimp one at a time into the egg wash and finally into the coconut, coating all over. Place the shrimp in the air-fryer basket and coat with cooking spray on both sides.

✦ Set the air fryer to 400°F (205°C) and cook for 10 minutes, or until the coconut is golden and the shrimp are pink and cooked through. *(Alternatively, heat a large sauté pan over medium heat, add a thin layer of oil, and sauté on both sides for 2 minutes or until coconut is golden. Or to cook in the oven, preheat your oven to broil. Place the shrimp on an oil-sprayed cooking rack and coat shrimp with cooking spray. Broil for 3 minutes on each side or until golden.)*

If you don't have eggs on hand, you can substitute ½ to ¾ cup (120 to 180 ml) buttermilk. Serve with your favorite bottled sauce including ketchup, chili sauce, BBQ sauce, or anything that tickles your fancy.

TO ENJOY LATER

After cooking, the shrimp can be cooled and refrigerated in an airtight container for up to 24 hours. To reheat, place the shrimp in an air fryer at 400°F (205°C) for 1 minute or in a preheated 350°F (175°C) oven for 4 to 5 minutes, or until crisp and heated through.

Crispy Salmon Burgers

1½ pounds (680 g) boneless, skinless salmon fillet, chopped into 1-inch (2.5 cm) chunks (*thawed if previously frozen*)

2 cloves garlic, grated

1-inch (2.5 cm) piece fresh ginger, peeled and grated

4 scallions, thinly sliced

1 tablespoon soy sauce

1 teaspoon spicy chili crisp or sambal oelek

1 teaspoon sesame oil

Kosher salt and freshly ground black pepper

½ cup (40 g) panko

Nonstick olive-oil cooking spray

I get excited just writing about this recipe. The key to these succulent salmon burgers is making sure you don't overprocess the fish in the food processor; you want larger chunks of fish so the burgers retain moisture during the cooking process.

+ Place half of the salmon in the bowl of a food processor. Add the garlic, ginger, scallions, soy sauce, chili crisp, and sesame oil. Season with salt and pepper.

+ Using the pulse function, process until the fish is in pea-size chunks. Add the remaining salmon and pulse 3 to 4 times, or until the mixture holds together when pressed in your hands, but large chunks of salmon remain.

+ Form the salmon mixture into four equal-size patties. Add the panko to a plate and coat each side of the salmon patties, pressing the panko gently to help it adhere.

+ Place a large nonstick skillet or coated cast-iron frying pan on the stovetop. Spritz the pan with an even layer of olive oil spray, then set over medium-high heat. Let it preheat for 1 minute, then add the salmon patties and cook for 4 minutes per side for medium, and 5 minutes per side for medium well.

These flavorful burgers are heavenly on their own, but I also like to serve them all dressed up on toasted brioche buns with a little Sriracha mayo and a handful of peppery arugula. Sigh.

TO ENJOY LATER

After cooking, the cooled burgers can be refrigerated in an airtight container for up to 2 days. To rewarm, microwave them for 45 seconds, place in a preheated 250°F (120°C) oven for 5 minutes, in an air fryer at 350°F (175°C) for 2 minutes, or in a sauté pan over low to medium heat for 1 to 2 minutes per side.

PREP IN ADVANCE

The uncooked burgers can be formed, covered, and refrigerated for up to 24 hours before cooking as directed. Or place the uncooked burgers on parchment-lined sheet pans, freeze for 1 to 2 hours, then transfer to labeled zip-top bags to freeze for up to 3 months. Defrost in the refrigerator overnight or for one hour at room temperature before cooking as directed.

Wild Mushroom Bean Bowl

2 tablespoons olive oil

1 shallot, thinly sliced

1 pound (455 g) shiitake, baby portobello, or other wild mushrooms, thinly sliced

Pinch crushed red pepper

4 cloves garlic, peeled

2 (15-ounce/140 g) cans white beans, drained and rinsed

½ cup (120 ml) vegetable broth or water

1 teaspoon kosher salt

Fresh ground black pepper

8 ounces (225 g) broccolini, broccoli rabe, or broccoli florets and stems, chopped

2 tablespoons sherry vinegar

Freshly shaved or grated Parmesan cheese

My husband deserves mention for his many pandemic bean bowl creations. Sensing the coming storm, one week prior to the lockdown he went to the grocery and returned with what seemed like one hundred cans of beans and was determined to creatively use them over the following months. No matter the vegetables in our fridge, he would come up with delectable variations depending on the season and what we had on hand, given our limited trips to the grocery store. This was one of our favorite combos, but be your own fridge forager and get creative coming up with a bean bowl that gets you jazzed.

◆ Heat the olive oil in a large sauté pan over medium heat. Sauté the shallots and mushrooms in the oil for 2 to 3 minutes. Add the crushed red pepper and garlic cloves and sauté for an additional minute, or until the mushrooms and garlic are just starting to turn golden. Remove the mushroom mixture and set it aside.

◆ Add the beans, broth, salt, and black pepper to taste to the sauté pan, bring to a boil, and use a fork to mash about half the beans. Reduce the heat to a simmer, add the broccoli, and cook for an additional 2 to 3 minutes, or until the broccoli is just fork tender. Return the mushrooms to the sauté pan, stir in the vinegar, and cook over medium heat for 1 minute, or until the mixture is heated through. Spoon into 4 bowls. Top with the Parmesan and serve.

If you have leftover rotisserie chicken or cooked shrimp or steak, you can add some right before serving. If you have tons of vegetables on hand, you can also add chopped cooked zucchini, cauliflower, asparagus, or anything you enjoy.

TO ENJOY LATER
The cooked bean mixture can be refrigerated in an airtight container for up to 3 days. To rewarm, microwave for 60 seconds or until heated through.

PREP TIME
15 minutes

COOK TIME
20 minutes

SERVES
4 to 6

Lemony White Bean Crunchy Salad

2 cups (90 g) 1-inch (2.5 cm) cubes bread (*French, ciabatta, or other favorite bread*)

3 tablespoons olive oil

2 tablespoons unsalted butter, melted

2 cloves garlic, chopped

1 teaspoon kosher salt

2 (15-ounce/430 g) cans white beans, drained and rinsed

1 shallot, thinly sliced

1 cup (145 g) cherry tomatoes, halved

2 cups (40 g) loosely packed arugula

Juice and zest of 1 lemon

This ain't your grandma's bean salad, or your supermarket's salad bar or school cafeteria's version either—all of which give me the willies. This one is from another universe. A better universe. Full of soft and creamy white beans, crunchy and garlicky homemade croutons, plus a big citrusy burst of lemon flavor throughout, this salad will destroy any less than positive notion you may have of what a bean salad can be, making it the ultimate picnic meal or dish you bring over to impress a friend.

✦ Preheat the oven to 350°F (175°C). Place the bread cubes on a baking sheet, drizzle with 2 tablespoons of the olive oil, and toss with the butter, garlic, and salt. Bake for 15 to 20 minutes, or until the bread is crunchy and golden.

✦ While the croutons bake, place the beans, shallot, cherry tomatoes, and arugula in a large bowl. Squeeze the lemon juice over the top, add the zest and the remaining 1 tablespoon olive oil, and toss to thoroughly coat. Add the hot croutons straight out of the oven and toss to combine.

Almost any raw vegetable—chopped cucumbers, bell peppers, fennel, and/ or canned artichokes or hearts of palm—will be magical in this salad. A handful of chopped fresh herbs like chervil, parsley, basil, chives, or dill would be a zippy addition too.

PREP IN ADVANCE

Croutons can be baked, cooled, and placed in zip-top bags up to 1 month before you need them. The prepped salad ingredients (the beans, shallot, cherry tomatoes, and arugula) can be combined and kept covered in the fridge for up to 3 days. Add the olive oil, lemon juice, and croutons just before serving.

PREP TIME
15 minutes

COOK TIME
30 minutes

SERVES
4 to 6

Mushroom, Spinach, and Pinto Bean Enchiladas

2 tablespoons olive oil

1 pound (455 g) mushrooms *(white, shiitake, or baby portobello)*, sliced

½ teaspoon garlic powder

1 teaspoon onion powder

½ teaspoon ground cumin powder

½ teaspoon kosher salt

2 cups (60 g) loosely packed fresh spinach

1 (15-ounce/430 g) can pinto beans, drained and rinsed

1½ cups (165 g) shredded Mexican blend cheese *(or a mix of Monterey Jack, mozzarella, and/or cheddar)*

1 (12-ounce/340 g) can enchilada sauce

6 large flour tortillas or 12 corn tortillas

These enchiladas are filling, super fun to make, and a proven crowd-pleaser. It's a richly flavored vegetarian dish that's perfect for kids and adults alike.

✦ Preheat the oven to 400°F (205°C).

✦ Heat the oil in a large sauté pan over medium heat. Add the mushrooms, garlic powder, onion powder, cumin, and salt to the oil and sauté, stirring occasionally, for 4 minutes or until the mushrooms start to turn golden. Add the spinach and stir until wilted, about 1 minute. Remove the mushrooms from the heat and stir in the beans and ½ cup (165 g) cheese.

✦ Spread half of the enchilada sauce in a 9 by 11-inch (23 by 28 cm) baking dish. Place the tortillas on a work surface. If you're using 9-inch (23 cm) flour tortillas, scoop ½ cup (120 ml) of the mushroom mixture onto the half of the tortilla closest to you. If you're using 6-inch (15 cm) corn tortillas, use a ¼ cup (60 ml) scoop. Roll up the tortillas and place them on top of the enchilada sauce. Top with the remaining enchilada sauce.

Cover the enchilada pans with foil and bake them for 15 minutes. Remove the foil, top with the remaining cup (110 g) of cheese, and bake for an additional 15 minutes. Allow to cool for a few minutes and then serve.

You can vary the type of beans used here. Black, navy, cannellini, great Northern, or red beans all work great.

I like to top these with fresh cilantro, sour cream, avocado slices, hot sauce, diced tomato, and more grated cheese.

TO ENJOY LATER
Cool enchiladas to room temperature and then refrigerate in an airtight container for up to 3 days. To rewarm, microwave each enchilada for 30 seconds, place in a preheated 250°F (120°C) oven for 5 minutes, or in an air fryer at 350°F (175°C) for 2 minutes.

PREP IN ADVANCE
Uncooked enchiladas can be covered in plastic wrap, and refrigerated for up to 1 day. To freeze, cover the dish with plastic wrap, then foil, label with date, and freeze for up to 3 months. When ready to eat, uncover and bake the enchiladas from frozen, adding an additional 5 minutes to the cooking time.

REPURPOSE LEFTOVERS
If you have any filling leftover, use it as filling for the Hand Pies (page 214).

PREP TIME
15 minutes

COOK TIME
36 minutes

MAKES
6 burgers

California Black Bean Burgers

2 (15-ounce/430 g) cans black beans, drained and rinsed

1 cup (55 g) cooked and drained riced cauliflower*

½ cup (55 g) chopped onion

½ cup (75 g) chopped red pepper

½ cup (60 g) masa harina

¼ cup (20 g) rolled oats

1 tablespoon tomato paste

1 teaspoon chili powder

1 teaspoon ground cumin

Zest of 1 lime

Pinch kosher salt and freshly ground black pepper

Nonstick cooking spray

FOR SERVING
6 buns

Green-leaf lettuce

2 avocados, peeled, pitted, and thinly sliced, or your favorite guacamole

Hot sauce of choice (optional)

I've tried ALL the store-bought vegetarian burgers out there, not to mention experimented with countless veggie burger recipes. So I feel confident saying that this is my hands-down favorite way to make them. The burgers are bound together by masa harina, aka corn flour, the same ingredient used to make tortillas. It gives these burgers a crisp exterior and a hearty texture. Swap in your favorite bean. Red, pinto, or black-eyed peas all work perfectly.

✦ Preheated the oven to 250°F (120°C).

✦ To the bowl of a food processor, add 1 can of the beans, the riced cauliflower, onion, red pepper, masa harina, oats, tomato paste, chile powder, cumin, lime zest, and a pinch of salt and black pepper. Pulse until mostly smooth and well combined, about 10 or 12 pulses. Add the remaining can of beans and pulse 3 or 4 times, or until mostly combined, but some texture remains.

✦ Use your hands to form the mixture into 6 equal-size patties. Spray a large nonstick skillet with olive oil spray and heat over medium heat for 1 minute. I typically cook 3 at a time so as not to crowd the burgers. Cook over medium-low heat for 8 minutes. Flip burgers and cook for an additional 8 minutes. Place burgers on a baking sheet in the preheated oven for up to 20 minutes while you cook the remaining burgers.

✦ Toast buns in your toaster or under the broiler. Serve burgers on toasted buns with lettuce, avocado slices, and hot sauce, if desired.

I use black beans here, but swap in your favorite. To cook the riced cauliflower, simply follow the directions on the package, then drain excess moisture before proceeding with the recipe.

TO ENJOY LATER

The cooked burgers can be cooled, stored in an airtight container, and refrigerated for up to 4 days. To rewarm, microwave for 45 seconds, place in a preheated to 250°F (120°C) oven for 5 minutes, or in an air fryer at 350°F (175°C) for 2 minutes.

PREP IN ADVANCE

The uncooked burgers can be arranged on a parchment-lined baking sheet to freeze for an hour, and then placed in labeled zip-top bags and frozen for up to 4 months. Defrost overnight and cook as directed.

PREP TIME
15 minutes

COOK TIME
35 minutes

MAKES
about 40 beanballs;
serves 4

Moroccan-Spiced Beanballs

2 (15.-ounce/445 g)
cans red kidney beans,
drained and rinsed

1 cup (100 g)
breadcrumbs

4 tablespoons
nutritional yeast

2 large eggs

2 teaspoons harissa
spice blend

1 teaspoon Kosher salt

3 tablespoons olive oil

1 onion, diced

2 cloves garlic, minced

1 (28-ounce/795 g) can
crushed tomatoes

2 teaspoons harissa
spice blend

1 teaspoon Kosher salt

¼ teaspoon freshly
ground black pepper

Juice of ½ lemon

Chopped fresh mint
and/or cilantro

Couscous, cooked
according to package
directions

Plain yogurt (optional)

Simmered in a sweet, but slightly spicy, Moroccan-inspired sauce, this easy dish comes together in a flash.

✦ To the bowl of a food processor, add the red beans, breadcrumbs, nutritional yeast, eggs, harissa, salt, and pepper. Pulse until the beans have broken down (but are not completely smooth), and the mixture is well combined, about 30 seconds.

✦ Using your hands, roll 1 tablespoon of the bean mixture into a ball. Repeat with the remaining mixture.

✦ Heat the olive oil in a large, deep nonstick skillet. Set over medium heat. Once shimmering, add the beanballs and cook for 1 to 2 minutes on each side, about 6 minutes total, or until golden. Remove to a plate and set aside.

✦ To the same skillet, add the onion and cook over medium heat for 4 minutes, or until it begins to soften. Add the garlic and cook for 30 seconds, then add the tomatoes, harissa, salt, and pepper and bring to a boil. Reduce to a simmer, cover, and cook for 15 minutes.

✦ Return the beanballs to the skillet and cook, covered, for 10 minutes, or until they are warmed through. Sprinkle with the lemon juice and mint, and serve over the prepared couscous with a drizzle of yogurt.

Add nutritional yeast here, and to any recipe that needs a boost of cheesy flavor (and B vitamins). P.S. It also takes popcorn to the next level.

Don't have a food processor? Simply mash the beans with a potato masher before combining with the rest of the ingredients.

A tablespoon-size cookie scoop is great for portioning out the mixture.

TO ENJOY LATER
The beanballs can be cooled and refrigerated in an airtight container with their sauce for up to 3 days.

PREP IN ADVANCE
Place uncooked balls on a parchment-lined baking sheet and freeze for an hour, then transfer to labeled zip-top bags and freeze up to 4 months. Cook from frozen as directed, adding 2 to 3 minutes to the cooking time.

REPURPOSE LEFTOVERS
Place any remaining warm or cooled beanballs and sauce in a hoagie or roll.

Butternut Squash and Chickpea Coconut Curry

2 tablespoons ghee or olive oil

3 whole cardamom pods

2 dried bay leaves

1 teaspoon cumin seeds

1 onion, diced

3 cloves garlic, minced

1 tablespoon minced fresh ginger

2 teaspoons ground turmeric

1 teaspoon garam masala

Kosher salt

1 tablespoon tomato paste

1 (28-ounce/795 g) can crushed tomatoes

4 cups cubed butternut squash (about 680 g/ 1½ pounds)

1 (14½-ounce/430-ml) can full-fat coconut milk

1 (14½-ounce/415 g) can chickpeas, drained and rinsed

Steamed jasmine rice, for serving

Chopped fresh cilantro, for serving

Few things are more comforting than a deeply flavorful bowl of curry, which is probably why this Indian-inspired rendition is so popular in my house. Vegetarians and carnivores alike, we all love this dish—it's one meal I can serve knowing everyone will be happy.

+ In a large, heavy-bottomed pot, heat the ghee over medium heat until shimmering. Add the cardamom pods, bay leaves, and cumin seeds and cook for 30 seconds to 1 minute, or until deeply fragrant.

+ Add the onion, garlic, and ginger to the pot and cook, stirring often, for 5 minutes, or until the onion begins to soften and take on some color. Add the turmeric, garam masala, and a pinch of salt and cook for 30 seconds. Add the tomato paste, stirring to evenly coat the onion with the paste. Deglaze the pan with 1 cup (240 ml) water, stirring up any brown bits that have formed on the bottom of the pot, and cook until reduced by half, about 3 minutes.

+ Pour in the crushed tomatoes and bring to a boil. Reduce heat to a simmer and cook for 8 to 10 minutes, then add the butternut squash and coconut milk and cook over medium-low heat for 15 minutes, or until the squash is tender.

+ Add the chickpeas and cook for 5 more minutes. Remove and discard the cardamom pods and bay leaves. Serve over the steamed rice with fresh cilantro.

I love the sweetness the butternut squash adds here, but you can easily replace it with cauliflower, sweet potatoes, or whatever hearty vegetable you have on hand.

TO ENJOY LATER

The curry can be cooled and refrigerated in an airtight container for up to 4 days. To freeze, let cool and then divide between glass jars or freezer bags, filled three-quarters full.

The Best Vegetarian Chili Evah!

1 tablespoon olive oil

1 yellow onion, diced

4 cloves garlic, minced

1 large carrot, diced

1 red, orange, or yellow bell pepper, diced

1 orange sweet potato, peeled and cut into ½-inch (12 mm) cubes

1 (4-ounce/115 g) can chopped mild chiles

1 (15-ounce/430 g) can white or pinto beans, rinsed and drained

1 (15-ounce/430 g) can black beans, rinsed and drained

1 (15-ounce/430 g) can kidney beans, rinsed and drained

2 (24-ounce/680 g) can chopped tomatoes (I use fire roasted)

1 cup frozen white shoepeg corn

2 bay leaves

1 tablespoon ground cumin

1 teaspoon chile powder

1 teaspoon paprika

1 teaspoon kosher salt

Freshly ground black pepper

Optional toppings: shredded cheese, fresh cilantro, sour cream, crushed tortilla chips, diced avocados, diced scallions, pumpkin seeds

Packed with tons of soluble fiber and just enough heat without being spicy, this chili has remained a treasured recipe in our family since I was a kid.

+ Heat the olive oil in a large pot over low-medium heat. Add the onion and cook for 4 minutes. Add the garlic and cook for an additional minute, or until the onion is translucent.

+ Add the carrot, bell pepper, sweet potato, chiles, three kinds of beans, tomatoes, frozen corn, bay leaves, cumin, chili powder, paprika, and 1 teaspoon salt plus black pepper to taste, and stir to combine. Bring to a boil, reduce the heat to a simmer, and cook for 45 minutes or until the vegetables are fork tender. *(Alternatively, toss everything in your slow cooker or Instant Pot and cook it for 4 hours on low. This recipe is happy cooking longer than directed to let the flavors fully meld.)*

TO ENJOY LATER

Chili can be cooled and refrigerated in an airtight container for up to 4 days. To freeze, divide the cooled chili among glass jars or freezer bags filled three-quarters full so they can expand when frozen for up to 4 months. Rewarm the chili in the microwave or in a pot over low to medium heat and pour over cooked pasta, rice, or your favorite grain.

Black Bean Brownie Cookies

PREP TIME
15 minutes, plus 30 minutes chill time

COOK TIME
24 minutes total (12 minutes per batch)

MAKES
14 cookies

1 cup (175 g) semisweet chocolate chips

½ cup (1 stick/115 g) unsalted butter

2 large eggs, at room temperature

½ cup (95 g) drained and rinsed black beans

½ cup (100 g) granulated sugar

½ cup (100 g) packed brown sugar

1 cup (125 g) all-purpose flour

¼ (35 g) cup cocoa powder

1 teaspoon baking powder

½ teaspoon kosher salt

¼ teaspoon instant espresso powder

Why ruin something so perfect as a brownie cookie by adding black beans? Cause it's delicious and you'll NEVER know they're there. I wouldn't go so far as to label these cookies as healthy, but they certainly pack a punch of protein and fiber that's the justification I always use for eating more of them.

✦ Add the chocolate chips and butter to a heat-safe bowl. Place a small pot of water on the stovetop and set the bowl of chocolate and butter on top to create a double boiler. Make sure the water does not come in contact with the bottom of the bowl. Set the heat to medium-low and cook until the butter and chocolate are completely melted, about 5 minutes. Remove from heat and set aside.

✦ Meanwhile, add the eggs, beans, and both sugars to the bowl of a food processor. Process until the beans are completely broken down and the eggs and sugar turn light and airy, about 3 to 4 minutes. Stream in the butter and chocolate mixture, pulsing until thoroughly incorporated.

✦ In a medium bowl, sift together the flour, cocoa powder, baking powder, salt, and espresso powder, then whisk to combine. Add the dry ingredients to the wet ingredients in the food processor and pulse just until the flour mixture has been absorbed. Scrape the batter back into the dry ingredients bowl, then cover and chill in the refrigerator for 30 minutes.

✦ Preheat the oven to 350°F (175°C) and line two rimmed sheet pans with parchment paper. Using a 3 tablespoon-size cookie scoop, scoop the cookie dough into balls and divide between prepared pans, leaving plenty of room for the cookies to spread. Bake one sheet at a time, turning the pan halfway through baking, for 12 minutes in all. Let cool on the sheet pan for 10 minutes before enjoying. Repeat with remaining sheet pan.

The key here is chill time. These cookies do not contain very much flour, so the dough needs time to cool in the fridge so it's solid enough to scoop, at least 30 minutes.

TO ENJOY LATER
The cookies can be cooled then refrigerated in an airtight container for up to 3 days. To freeze, place the cooled cookies in labeled zip-top bags and freeze for up to 4 months. To rewarm, microwave for 30 seconds, place in a preheated 250°F (120°C) oven for 3 minutes, or in an air fryer at 350°F (175°C) for 1 minute.

PREP TIME
10 minutes

COOK TIME
20 minutes

SERVES
4 to 6

Kitchen Sink Pasta

Kosher salt

1 pound (455 g) pasta shape of choice

2 tablespoons olive oil

1 small yellow onion, diced

1 cup (about 70 g) raw or cooked chopped vegetables of choice (*mushrooms, zucchini, scallions, broccoli, cauliflower, spinach, kale, bell peppers, etc.*)

1 pound (455 g) ground or chopped meat of choice (*rotisserie or roast chicken, ground beef or turkey, kielbasa*), cooked (about 1½ cups)

1 (25-ounce/710 g) jar marinara sauce

Freshly ground black pepper

½ cup (50 g) grated Parmesan, or 1 cup (110 g) grated mozzarella

Toppings: fresh basil, grated Parmesan, mozzarella, or crushed red pepper

Since I do my shopping every Sunday, by the following weekend our refrigerator begins to look bare. Our family turned Saturday nights into a game—fridge foraging and then using what we find to whip up a creative meal. Pasta is one of the best canvases to adorn with leftovers or a bit of this or that to make a satisfying, fast, seasonal dish that we can all share credit for.

✦ Heat a large pot of salted water to a boil. Add the pasta and cook according to package directions.

✦ Heat a large pot over medium heat. Add the olive oil and salt and sauté the onion for 3 minutes. Add the remaining vegetables. Sauté for 3 minutes if raw and 1 minute if cooked.

✦ Add the cooked meat, marinara sauce, salt, and black pepper to taste and cook for an additional 2 to 3 minutes or until heated through.

✦ Drain the water from the pasta, reserving ½ cup. Pour the cooked pasta into the marinara mixture and stir to combine. Stir in the cheese and transfer the pasta into a large serving bowl. Top with additional cheese, fresh herbs, and/or crushed red pepper.

Don't have marinara sauce? Homemade or prepared pesto (page 132) works like a dream. Have cream on hand? Pour in ¼ cup when you add the marinara for a richer sauce.

TO ENJOY LATER
After the pasta cooks, cool and refrigerate it in an airtight container for up to 3 days. Serve at room temperature or microwave for 30 seconds.

REPURPOSE LEFTOVERS
Sauté double the vegetables to use for another meal. Add the extra half to the Quesadillas (page 227), Any Veggie Frittata (page 60), or on top of salads.

Blistered Cherry Tomato and Gooey Mozzarella Spaghetti

⅓ cup (75 ml) olive oil

1 shallot, thinly sliced

4 cloves garlic, thinly sliced

2 pounds (910 g) cherry tomatoes

⅓ cup (75 ml) white wine

Kosher salt and freshly ground black pepper

Pinch crushed red pepper

1 pound (455 g) spaghetti

2 tablespoons Cheesy Compound Butter (page 135) or plain unsalted butter

½ cup (50 g) grated Parmesan cheese

8 ounces (225 g) fresh mozzarella, torn or cut into bite-size pieces

8 to 10 fresh basil leaves, cut into thin ribbons

This is just about the easiest tomato sauce you'll ever make, and when made with ripe summer tomatoes, the flavor is hard to beat. I love using cherry tomatoes because they require no extra chopping, but you can make this sauce with any tomatoes you have on hand; just slice them into bite-size pieces first.

+ To blister the tomatoes, heat the olive oil in a large nonstick or coated cast-iron skillet over medium-low heat. Add the shallots and garlic and cook over low heat until they begin to soften and smell very fragrant, about 5 minutes. Add the tomatoes, wine, a pinch of salt, black pepper to taste, and a pinch of crushed red pepper. Cover and cook for 10 minutes.

+ Bring a large pot of salted water to a boil. Add the pasta and cook to al dente, according to package directions. Drain and set aside.

+ Once the tomatoes have cooked for 10 minutes, uncover the pan and mash the tomatoes with a potato masher or the back of a fork until broken down.

+ Simmer the sauce, uncovered, for 5 minutes, then remove from heat and add the cooked pasta and compound butter and toss until the butter is melted. Stir in the Parmesan, mozzarella, and basil, tossing to combine and slightly melt the mozzarella cheese.

This sauce isn't just for pasta. You can also use it to top chicken paillard, sautéed or baked fish, even leftover rice or grains.

PREP IN ADVANCE
The tomato sauce can be prepared up to 2 days ahead, cooled, and placed in an airtight container. When ready to prepare, bring sauce to a simmer and proceed as directed.

REPURPOSE LEFTOVERS
Double the blistered cherry tomatoes and remove half from the pot. Mash and simmer into a sauce, and then place on top of cooked chicken or fish.

PREP TIME
15 minutes

COOK TIME
40 minutes

SERVES
4 to 6

Broccolini and Crispy White Bean Pasta

with PANCETTA AND LEMON

2 tablespoons olive oil

4 ounces (115 g) diced pancetta

2 bunches broccolini, ends trimmed and discarded, stalks cut in half widthwise

1 (14½-ounce/415 g) can white beans

3 cloves garlic, thinly sliced

1 shallot, thinly sliced

Kosher salt and freshly ground black pepper

Crushed red pepper

1 pound (455 g) pasta of your choice

⅓ cup (75 ml) dry white wine

Juice and zest of 1 lemon

1 cup (100 g) freshly grated Parmesan cheese, plus more for serving

This hearty meal is pretty much effortless to make. Toss all of the ingredients on a sheet pan, roast until crisp, then toss with cooked pasta, a hit of lemon, and lots of Parmesan cheese for an easy weeknight meal with minimal cleanup!

✦ Preheat the oven to 425°F (220°C). Add about half of the olive oil to a rimmed sheet pan, then add the pancetta, broccolini, white beans, garlic, and shallot to the pan. Season with salt, black pepper, and crushed red pepper to taste. Add the remaining tablespoon olive oil, then toss well so everything is evenly coated.

✦ Roast for about 20 minutes, then stir well and roast for an additional 20 minutes, or until the pancetta and beans are crisp and the broccoli is tender.

✦ While the broccoli mixture roasts, bring a large pot of salted water to a boil. Add the pasta and cook until al dente. Reserve about 1 cup (240 ml) pasta water and set aside. Drain the pasta and return it to the pot.

✦ Remove the sheet pan from the oven and add the white wine, scraping up any brown bits on the bottom of the pan. Scrape the mixture into the pot of pasta, then add the lemon juice and zest. Add the Parmesan cheese and about ½ cup (120 ml) of the pasta water and stir until the cheese starts to melt and form a creamy sauce, adding more pasta water if needed.

✦ Divide among 4 pasta bowls and top each portion with a bit more Parmesan cheese before serving.

Don't dump that pasta water! It's filled with all kinds of goodness (e.g., starch!) that will make this dreamy sauce extra creamy sans extra dairy.

TO ENJOY LATER
Cool and refrigerate the pasta in an airtight container for up to 3 days. Serve at room temperature or reheat in a microwave for 30 seconds, mixing in a little hot water to loosen the sauce.

REPURPOSE LEFTOVERS
Double the broccoli-bean-pancetta mixture. Remove half of the mixture after roasting and serve at another meal alongside a cooked protein, like chicken or fish.

Easy Ricotta Gnocchi

PREP TIME
20 minutes

COOK TIME
5 minutes

SERVES
2 to 4

GNOCCHI

½ teaspoon kosher salt, plus more for boiling gnocchi

1½ cups (150 g) grated Parmesan cheese

1 cup (245 g) firm ricotta cheese

2 large egg yolks

1 tablespoon olive oil

1 cup (125 g) all-purpose flour, plus more for rolling

FOR SERVING

2 tablespoons Lemon-Herb Compound Butter (page 135), or plain unsalted butter

Freshly grated Parmesan cheese

Flaky salt

This recipe requires zero special equipment, no resting time, and only a handful of ingredients. You're going to want to make it *often*.

✦ Bring a large pot of salted water to a boil. In a medium bowl, add the Parmesan, ricotta, egg yolks, and olive oil and mix with a fork until well combined. Sprinkle the flour and salt on top, and stir with the fork to gently combine. When the mixture gets too thick to mix with a fork, use your hands to form the dough into a disk.

✦ Place the dough on a wooden surface lightly dusted with flour. Line a rimmed sheet pan with parchment paper, then dust it with flour. Cut the disk into 4 equal-size portions and roll each portion into a long rope, about ½ inch (12 mm) in diameter. Using a bench scraper, cut the rope into ½- to 1-inch (12 mm to 2.5 cm) segments. Place on the prepared sheet pan and toss gently to coat in flour to prevent sticking. Repeat with the remaining dough.

✦ When all the gnocchi have been formed, add the compound butter to a large nonstick skillet. Set over low heat and gently melt while starting the next step.

✦ Add the gnocchi to the boiling water and cook until they all float to the surface, about 3 minutes. Remove them with a spider strainer (save the cooking liquid) and transfer the gnocchi directly into the pan of melted butter. Toss to coat, then gently stir in about ¼–½ cup (120 ml) of the reserved pasta water, until a thick and luscious sauce forms.

✦ Serve topped with grated Parmesan cheese and flaky salt.

Handle the dough as little as possible to ensure you wind up with light and fluffy gnocchi. So don't worry about rolling the dough into perfect cylinders; less is more—taste is more important than looks!

I keep it simple, topping it with just a dollop of compound butter (page 135), but pesto (page 132), marinara, a brown butter sauce, or béchamel would be glorious too.

TO ENJOY LATER
The cooked gnocchi in its sauce can be refrigerated in an airtight container for up to 2 days. Reheat in the microwave.

PREP IN ADVANCE
Gently place uncooked gnocchi in airtight containers and refrigerate for up to 3 days. To freeze, place the uncooked gnocchi on a parchment-lined baking sheet, freeze for one hour, and then transfer gnocchi into labeled zip-top bags and freeze for up to 4 months. Cook as directed above, adding 30 seconds to the cooking time.

PREP TIME
5 minutes

COOK TIME
8 minutes

MAKES
6 rice cakes

Cheesy Brown Rice Cakes

2 cups (390 g) cooked brown rice *(or any type of leftover rice)*

2 large eggs, whisked

½ cup (112 g) grated mozzarella, cheddar, Gruyère, or provolone cheese

¼ teaspoon kosher salt

Olive, canola, avocado, or vegetable oil

Keeping leftover rice of any kind in my fridge is one of my most treasured meal prep hacks. I'm sure you can think of the usual suspect recipes (like fried rice) for making a quick, last-minute meal, but there is another world of amazing things you can do with this humble grain. These crunchy cakes in their cheesy, savory form have long been one of my kids' most beloved weeknight meals. During the pandemic, my husband came up with a sweet version that's equally at home as breakfast, dessert, or a late-night snack. Either way you make them, you need these cakes in your recipe arsenal!

✦ Place the rice, eggs, cheese, and salt in a bowl and stir until thoroughly combined.

✦ Heat a large skillet over medium-high heat and add a thin layer of oil. Using an ice cream scoop or ¼ cup (60 ml) measure, scoop 4 portions of the rice mixture and place in the skillet with space between them. Use a spatula to gently press down into a 1-inch-thick patty. Cook for 4 minutes on each side, or until golden and crispy on both sides.

For sweet rice cakes, omit the cheese and add 2 tablespoons brown or coconut sugar, 1 teaspoon ground cinnamon, and 1 teaspoon vanilla extract. Cook as directed and top with maple syrup and fresh fruit to serve.

TO ENJOY LATER

The cooked rice cakes can be cooled and refrigerated in an airtight container for up to 4 days. To rewarm, microwave for 30 seconds, place in an air fryer at 350°F (175°C) for 3 minutes, or sauté on the stovetop for 1 minute on each side.

PREP IN ADVANCE

The rice pancake mixture can be made, covered, and refrigerated for up to 24 hours before sautéing as directed.

Leftover Rice Pudding

2 cups (390 g) cooked rice *(any type of rice works)*

2 cups (480 ml) whole milk

3 tablespoons sugar

1 large egg, whisked

Pinch kosher salt

1 teaspoon vanilla extract

Optional toppings: whipped cream; ground cinnamon; fresh berries; sliced banana; raisins or other dried fruits; shaved chocolate; coconut flakes; chopped walnuts, almonds, or cashews; thin ribbons of fresh mint or basil (roll up and slice crosswise)

One basic cooking rule of thumb in our house: If you're making rice, double it because it's one of the best things you can have on hand in the fridge. While people often think of utilizing rice in savory dishes, some of the recipes I love use it for sweet ones. Rice is a true chameleon. It's the perfect culinary pairing to almost anything you can think of and this leftover pudding is a great example of that. Serve it for breakfast or dessert and top it with anything you choose in your pantry, from dried or fresh fruits to spices, chocolate, coconut, and more.

Place the cooked rice and 1½ cups (360 ml) of the milk in a saucepan and bring to a boil. Reduce the heat to a simmer and cook, whisking occasionally, for 15 minutes. Add the remaining ½ cup (120 ml) milk, the sugar, egg, and salt and cook for 3 to 5 minutes, stirring occasionally, until the rice pudding is thick and creamy. Remove from the heat and stir in the vanilla. The pudding will continue to thicken as it sets. Divide among 4 bowls and sprinkle with desired toppings.

I generally don't have the patience to wait before getting a bowlful of this pudding in my tummy (yes, it's also delicious warm), but if you can resist, refrigerate it for a few hours first to cool and firm it up. Have it for breakfast, pop a jar into a lunch box, or enjoy it for dessert.

TO ENJOY LATER
The pudding can be cooled and refrigerated for up to 3 days. It can be rewarmed in the microwave for 30 seconds, but truth be told, cold rice pudding is my go-to.

PREP IN ADVANCE
Cook the rice at the beginning of the week, ideally when making another recipe that calls for rice, then cool and refrigerate it in an airtight container, so you can make leftover rice pudding for dessert another day.

Go-To Bibimbap

4 tablespoons gochujang sauce

4 tablespoons plus 4 teaspoons toasted sesame oil

2 teaspoons rice or apple cider vinegar

2 teaspoons granulated or brown sugar

8 cloves garlic, minced

1 pound (455 g) ribeye, beef tenderloin, or other thick steak, thinly sliced

1 tablespoon plus 2 teaspoons low-sodium soy sauce or tamari

Vegetable, canola, avocado, or olive oil

1 cup (90 g) thinly sliced shiitake mushrooms

1 cup (125 g) bean sprouts

Kosher salt

1½ cups (45 g) loosely packed fresh spinach

1 large carrot, shredded or sliced into thin batons

4 large eggs

4 cups (790 g) warm cooked white or brown rice

FOR SERVING
Kimchi

2 scallions (white and green parts), thinly sliced (optional)

Toasted sesame seeds, (optional)

Bibimbap is a Korean dish that translates to "mixed rice," and it's as fun to make as it is to eat. You can serve any leftover cooked meat and vegetables on rice with this sauce.

✦ In a small bowl, whisk together the gochujang, 2 tablespoons sesame oil, the cider, sugar, 2 tablespoons water, and 2 cloves minced garlic in a small bowl.

✦ Place the beef, 4 cloves minced garlic, 1 tablespoons soy sauce, and 1 tablespoon sesame oil in a bowl and let the beef marinate at room temperature while you prep the other ingredients.

✦ Heat a large sauté pan over medium heat. Add 1 tablespoon vegetable oil and sauté the mushrooms for 3 to 4 minutes, or until they start to turn golden. Add the remaining 2 cloves of minced garlic and 2 teaspoons soy sauce and stir for 30 seconds. Remove to a plate.

✦ Add the bean sprouts, a pinch of salt, and 1 teaspoon sesame oil to the pan and sauté for 1 to 2 minutes, or until just starting to soften. Remove to a plate.

✦ Add the spinach, a pinch of salt, and 1 teaspoon toasted sesame oil to the same pan over medium and sauté for 1 to 2 minutes or until just starting to soften. Remove to a plate.

CONTINUES

+ Add 1 tablespoon vegetable oil to the pan. Add the carrots and a pinch of salt and sauté for 2 minutes, or until starting to soften. Remove to a plate.

+ Raise heat to medium-high heat and sauté the beef mixture for 4 to 5 minutes, or until the meat is starting to turn golden. Remove to a plate.

+ Rinse out the pan and place it over medium heat. Coat the pan with oil, gently crack the eggs into the pan, and sprinkle with ½ teaspoon salt or to taste. If your pan isn't large enough to fit 4 eggs, this can be done in two stages. Cook the eggs sunny side up for 3 minutes, or until the edges are just starting to turn golden.

+ Divide the warmed rice among 4 bowls, add the vegetables and beef, and place a cooked egg on top. Garnish with the bibimbap sauce, kimchi, scallions, and sesame seeds, if desired.

Have frozen steak? Allow the steak to defrost for 1 hour and slice it into thin pieces while still super cold (frozen steak is much easier to slice than fresh). Want to make this bibimbap vegetarian? Slice a block of tofu into 32 cubes. Heat a large sauté pan with olive oil over medium heat and sauté the tofu for 5 to 6 minutes, shaking the pan occasionally to brown the sides evenly or until several sides are golden. Season with salt and pepper or favorite seasoning to taste.

PREP IN ADVANCE

All of the components, minus the egg, can be cooked the day before assembling the bowl, and then reheated before serving.

PREP TIME
25 minutes

COOK TIME
1 hour 40 minutes

SERVES
4 to 6

Stuffed Peppers

2 tablespoons olive oil, plus more for the baking dish

4 red, orange, yellow, or green bell peppers, halved and cored, seeds and ribs discarded

1 cup (190 g) green lentils, rinsed

Kosher salt

1 cup (195 g) white or brown rice, rinsed

½ onion, diced

2 cloves garlic, minced

1 small zucchini, grated

1 teaspoon dried oregano

1 tablespoon tomato paste

1 cup (240 ml) vegetable broth

1 cup (240 ml) marinara sauce

Freshly ground black pepper

1 cup (110 g) low-moisture shredded mozzarella

½ cup (50 g) grated Parmesan cheese

Chopped fresh parsley, for garnish (optional)

Lentils don't often appear in stuffed pepper recipes but after trying this version you will agree they should. They provide a plant-based protein and meaty texture, setting this stuffed pepper apart from the rest.

✦ Preheat the oven to 400°F (205°C). Coat a 9 by 13-inch (23 by 33 cm) baking dish with olive oil, then place the pepper halves in the pan, cut side up.

✦ Bring 4 cups (about 1 liter) water to a boil. Add the lentils and reduce heat to a simmer. Cook for 30 minutes, or until tender. Drain the excess water and set lentils aside. To prepare the rice, bring 1¾ cups (420 ml) water and a pinch of salt to a boil in a small saucepan. Add the rice, reduce to a simmer and cook over low heat until the water has been absorbed and the rice is tender and fluffy, about 15 minutes (for brown rice, cook for 35 to 40 minutes or according to package directions). Remove from the heat and let sit for 5 minutes before fluffing with a fork.

✦ Heat the olive oil in a large sauté pan over medium heat. Once shimmering, add the onion and cook for 5 minutes, or until softened. Add the garlic and zucchini and cook for 5 minutes. Add the oregano and tomato paste and cook, stirring often, for 2 minutes.

✦ Add the cooked lentils and rice to the sauté pan, then stir in ½ cup (120 ml) of the vegetable broth and the marinara sauce. Season with salt and black pepper and cook for 3 to 5 minutes.

✦ Divide the lentil and rice mixture among the pepper halves, then pour around the peppers the remaining ½ cup (120 ml) broth into the baking dish, cover with foil, and bake for 40 minutes.

✦ Remove from the oven, uncover, then sprinkle the mozzarella and Parmesan evenly over the peppers. Return to the oven for 10 to 15 minutes, or until the cheese is melted. Sprinkle with parsley, if desired.

At the end of the baking time, you may be surprised to find a lot of liquid in the dish. Don't worry, the liquid is released by the peppers as they cook down!

If you have wild rice, black rice, or another variety in your pantry, you can use it in place of the white or brown rice.

TO ENJOY LATER

Allow stuffed peppers to cool and refrigerate for up to 4 days. To rewarm, microwave for 60 seconds each, place in a preheated 250°F (120°C) oven for 7 to 8 minutes, or in an air fryer at 350°F (175°C) for 3 minutes.

PREP IN ADVANCE

Cover the pan of uncooked stuffed peppers with plastic and refrigerate for up to 24 hours before baking. Or cover the plastic-wrapped baking dish with foil and label with tape using a marker. Freeze for up to 4 months. Bake as directed, adding 5 minutes to the total bake time to bake from frozen, or defrost in the fridge overnight.

PREP TIME
15 minutes

COOK TIME
50 minutes

SERVES
4 to 6

Wild Rice and Mushroom Soup

2 tablespoons olive oil

1 pound (455 g) cremini mushrooms, sliced

1 pound (455 g) shiitake mushrooms, stems discarded, caps sliced

Kosher salt and freshly ground black pepper

1 onion, diced

1 shallot, minced

2 carrots, diced

2 stalks celery, diced

1 teaspoon dried thyme

½ cup (120 ml) dry white wine

1 cup (180 g) wild rice blend

5 cups (1.2 L) vegetable broth

1 cup (240 ml) canned coconut milk

¼ cup (13 g) chopped fresh flat- or curly-leaf parsley, or 1 tablespoon fresh thyme, chopped

Long on savoriness, this soup is creamy and hearty, thanks to coconut milk and protein-packed wild rice. Plus, the shiitakes and cremini mushrooms add amazing umami flavor and lend a meaty texture.

+ Set an electric pressure cooker or Instant Pot to the sauté function and add 1 tablespoon of the olive oil. Cook the cremini mushrooms in the oil for 10 minutes, stirring occasionally, or until brown. Remove with a slotted spoon and set aside. Add the shiitake mushrooms and cook for 10 minutes, stirring occasionally, or until brown. Remove with a slotted spoon and set aside. Season the mushrooms with salt and pepper.

+ Add the remaining 2 tablespoons olive oil to the pressure cooker. Once shimmering, sauté the onion, shallot, carrots, celery, and thyme for 5 minutes, or until the onions begin to soften. Season with salt and pepper. Pour in the wine and cook until reduced by half, about 2 minutes. Turn off the sauté function.

+ Add the rice, mushrooms, and broth to the pressure cooker; cover and close the valve to seal. Cook at high pressure for 15 minutes, then release pressure manually by opening the valve. Open the top, pour in the coconut milk, and set to sauté for 5 minutes. Turn off the pressure cooker and stir in the parsley before serving. *(Alternatively, if you don't have an electric pressure cooker, you can make this on the stovetop in a large Dutch oven. Follow the directions above and, after adding the stock and rice, simply cover the pot and cook the soup over low heat for about 50 minutes, or until the rice is tender. Then stir in the coconut milk and warm through before serving. You can also use a slow cooker after sautéing the mushrooms. Place on high heat for 4 hours.)*

This is the recipe to use a variety of wild mushrooms (using a cloth or paper towel to clean them), including king trumpet, oyster, or maitake. They add umami and a meaty texture.

TO ENJOY LATER

Allow soup to cool and refrigerate in an airtight container for up to 4 days. To freeze, fill glass jars or freezer bags three-quarters full so the soup can expand when frozen, and freeze for up to 4 months. Defrost the soup in the microwave or in a pot over low to medium heat.

Overnight Flight (of Oats), Five Ways

1 cup (90 g) rolled oats

1 cup (240 ml) milk of choice

1 cup (240 ml) plain Greek yogurt

3 tablespoons honey

Every time I see overnight oats at Starbucks or in the grocery for five dollars or more I'm perplexed. There are few recipes that are easier (or more economical) to prepare at home. You can make an entire batch of this nutritious delight for a fraction of the cost of what you'd pay for one in the store. This recipe entails dumping, stirring, dividing, and then topping with whatever your heart desires. I suggest some flavor options below, but the fun here is getting creative and making a bunch of different kinds. I stack up a line of jars in the fridge so my family can grab whatever looks most appealing for a breakfast or snack that tastes just as good at the kitchen table as it does on the go.

✦ Whisk together the oats, milk, yogurt, and honey in a medium bowl. Stir in any of your preferred add-ins to add flavor and natural color.

✦ Divide the overnight oat mixture between four 8-ounce (225 g) jars or cups, cover, and refrigerate for 2 hours to overnight before serving.

FLAVOR OPTIONS

1. **Blueberry Overnight Oats:** Stir in ½ cup (145 g/155 g) fresh or frozen blueberries.

2. **Strawberry Overnight Oats:** Stir in ½ cup (145 g/150 g) fresh or frozen diced strawberries.

3. **Coffee Overnight Oats:** Stir in 2 tablespoons instant coffee.

4. **Almond Butter Overnight Oats:** Stir in ¼ cup (60 ml) creamy or crunchy almond butter.

5. **Passion fruit Overnight Oats:** Stir in the juice and seeds of 2 passion fruit.

You can use any type of yogurt you enjoy, but I love the tang, neutral flavor, and extra protein from Greek yogurt. Having said that, I've made this with raspberry and vanilla yogurt and it's just as luscious and flavorful.

TO ENJOY LATER
Oats can be refrigerated in covered containers for up to 3 days with fruit toppings and up to 5 with other toppings.

PREP TIME
5 minutes

COOK TIME
20 minutes

SERVES
4 to 6

Apple Cinnamon Steel-Cut Oatmeal

1½ cups (235 g) steel-cut oats

1 cup (240 ml) whole milk or plant-based milk of choice

2 apples, cored and diced

½ cup (110 g) packed brown sugar

2 tablespoons Cinnamon-Sugar Compound Butter (page 135), or regular butter and 2 teaspoons ground cinnamon

½ teaspoon kosher salt

Optional toppings: chopped pecans or walnuts, fresh berries, pure maple syrup, milk of choice

Getting dinner organized for the week gives me a sense of pride and accomplishment, but if I can summon the bandwidth, there is something about also preparing breakfast for the week ahead that just makes me feel like superwoman. Having something filling and nutritious ready to go makes my day run a bit more smoothly and, especially after the last few years we've all experienced, who doesn't need that?

✦ Add the oats, milk, 3 cups (720 ml) water, the apples, brown sugar, butter, cinnamon if needed, and salt to an electric pressure cooker. Cover and set the valve to seal. Cook at high pressure for 5 minutes, then let the pressure release naturally for 15 minutes.

✦ Release any remaining pressure manually, then stir the oats to combine all the ingredients and serve with any of the toppings, if using. *(Alternatively, if you do not have a pressure cooker, you can make this on the stovetop. Simply bring the milk and 4 cups [960 ml] water to a boil in a medium pot. Stir in the oats, apples, brown sugar, butter, and salt and reduce heat to a simmer. Cook for about 30 minutes, or until tender. To make in a slow cooker, place all of the ingredients in the slow cooker and cook on low for 4 hours to overnight. To cook in a rice cooker, add all the ingredients to the rice cooking container and cook on the "Porridge" setting.)*

If you don't have the cinnamon-sugar compound butter on hand, use regular butter and add 2 teaspoons of cinnamon to the oats before cooking.

TO ENJOY LATER

The cooked oatmeal can be cooled and then refrigerated in an airtight container for up to 4 days, or frozen in individual portions in airtight containers for up to 4 months. Defrost in the refrigerator overnight. To reheat, microwave for 1 minute, or place in a pot over low heat, adding a little water or milk to loosen, for 2 to 3 minutes, or until warmed through.

Chocolate and Cherry Baked Oats

Butter or nonstick cooking spray, for the ramekins

1 cup (90 g) rolled oats

1 large egg

1 large banana

¾ cup (180 ml) milk of choice

2 tablespoons pure maple syrup or honey

2 tablespoons unsweetened cocoa powder

1 teaspoon baking powder

⅛ teaspoon kosher salt

2 tablespoons dried cherries

4 tablespoons (45 g) semisweet or bittersweet chocolate chunks or chips

It's a miracle that I don't break a sweat during my morning routine, because from the second I wake it's go go go! When I need something warm, filling, and simple for breakfast, I jump out of bed, turn on the oven, toss most of the ingredients in the blender, divide the mixture into ramekins, and top with dried cherries and chunks of chocolate (always appropriate for breakfast in my book). While I'm getting myself and the kids ready, the oats bake up puffy and golden, and 20 minutes or so later, breakfast is served.

✦ Preheat the oven to 350°F (175°C). Coat four 6-ounce (180 ml) ramekins with butter or cooking spray.

✦ In a blender, place the oats, egg, banana, milk, maple syrup, cocoa powder, baking powder, and salt and puree for 30 seconds or until smooth. Stir in the dried cherries and 2 tablespoons of the chocolate chips. Sprinkle the ramekins with the remaining 2 tablespoons chips and bake for 20 to 25 minutes or until puffed and golden. *(Alternatively, this recipe can be microwaved for 2 minutes or cooked in an air fryer set at 350°F [175°C] for 10 to 12 minutes or until bubbling.)*

If you don't have bananas on hand, ½ cup applesauce works too.

TO ENJOY LATER
The baked oats can be cooled, covered, and then refrigerated for up to 3 days. To rewarm, microwave for 30 seconds, place in a preheated 250°F (120°C) oven for 5 minutes, or in an air fryer at 350°F (175°C) for 2 minutes.

PREP IN ADVANCE
Before baking, divide the oat mixture between ramekins and refrigerate for up to 3 days or until ready to bake.

Peanut Butter and Chocolate Olive Oil Granola

PREP TIME
10 minutes

COOK TIME
30 minutes

MAKES
about 8 cups (120 g);
16 servings

¾ cup (180 ml) creamy all-natural peanut butter

½ cup (120 ml) olive oil

½ cup (120 ml) pure maple syrup

1 tablespoon vanilla extract

4 cups (360 g) rolled oats

1 cup (85 g) unsweetened coconut flakes

1 cup (150 g) dry-roasted unsalted peanuts

½ teaspoon kosher salt

½ teaspoon ground cinnamon

1 cup (175 g) semisweet or dark chocolate chips or chunks

I'll take any excuse I can to enjoy peanut butter and chocolate for breakfast. This not-too-sweet granola sort of tastes like a peanut butter cup, and who doesn't want that to kick off the day?

✦ Preheat the oven to 350°F (175°C) and line a rimmed sheet pan with parchment paper.

✦ Place the peanut butter in a large, microwave-safe bowl and heat in microwave for about 30 seconds, or until soft and runny. Whisk in the olive oil, maple syrup, and vanilla extract until smooth.

✦ To the same bowl, add the oats, coconut, peanuts, salt, and cinnamon and stir until all of the oats are evenly coated in the peanut butter mixture.

✦ Spread onto the prepared sheet pan in an even layer. Bake for 30 to 35 minutes, stirring the granola every 10 minutes or so to ensure it cooks evenly. Remove from the oven when the granola feels dry to the touch and is golden in color.

✦ Let cool on the pan for 30 minutes, then scatter the chocolate chips on top. Let fully cool for 1 hour, or until the granola easily breaks into chunks.

TO ENJOY LATER

Store the granola in an airtight container at room temperature for up to one week, or in the freezer in labeled zip-top bags for up to 3 months. Serve on top of Greek yogurt or ice cream.

PREP TIME
10 minutes

CHILL TIME
1 hour

COOK TIME
18 to 20 minutes

MAKES
12 cookies

Chocolate Granola Breakfast Cookies

2 cups (180 g) old-fashioned oats *(gluten-free oats work too)*

1 banana, mashed

¼ cup (60 ml) pumpkin or apple butter

1 cup (240 ml) nut or seed butter *(preferably almond, peanut, cashew, or sun butter)*

¼ cup (60 ml) pure maple syrup, honey, or agave nectar

¼ cup (35 g) unsweetened cacao powder

1 teaspoon ground cinnamon

½ teaspoon kosher salt

1 tablespoon chia or hemp seeds

½ cup (60 g) granola of choice *(Peanut Butter and Chocolate Olive Oil Granola, page 203, or favorite store-bought option)*

½ cup (85 g) semisweet or dark chocolate chips or chunks

My chocolate granola obsession has become a real problem. I don't remember when or why it began, but what started as a handful (or two, sometimes three) every day has, recently, been known to turn into almost an entire bag—or batch of my homemade version. I prefer big clumps of granola, which means I usually end up with a cup or so of the smaller pieces, and this recipe is where I use them. Not only do these cookies make use of these finer pieces of granola and pack a ton of crunch, but I double down on the chocolate (I'm a firm believer that you can never have too much chocolate). The fact that a cookie can legitimately qualify as a healthy breakfast (and a quick grab-and-go one at that) always comes as welcome news to everyone in my house, especially the younger members.

+ Preheat the oven to 325°F (165°C).

+ In the bowl of a standing mixer or in a large bowl if you're using a hand mixer, place the oats, banana, pumpkin butter, nut butter, maple syrup, cacao powder, cinnamon, salt, and chia seeds. Mix until thoroughly combined and oats are no4589 longer dry. Refrigerate the dough for 1 hour to overnight.

+ Scoop ¼-cup (32 g) portions onto a parchment- or silpat-lined baking sheet, leaving space between them. Using your palm or the bottom of a glass, press the cookies down to make them about ½ inch (12 mm) thick.

+ Bake for 18 to 20 minutes or until slightly golden. Allow to cool on the baking sheet completely.

The cookies can be formed into scoops and placed on parchment or Silpat-lined baking sheets in the refrigerator for up to 2 days before baking, or frozen and placed in zip-top bags for up to 4 months.

TO ENJOY LATER

After baking, place the cooled cookies in airtight containers or labeled zip-top bags for up to 2 days at room temperature or refrigerate for up to 5 days. Or the cookies can be cooled and divided among glass jars or labeled freezer bags and frozen for up to 4 months.

PREP TIME
15 minutes

COOK TIME
18 to 20 minutes

MAKES
8 scones

Scones, Four Ways

2¼ cups (280 g) all-purpose flour

⅓ cup (65 g) sugar

2 tablespoons baking powder

6 tablespoons (85 g) unsalted butter, chilled

1 large egg

1 teaspoon vanilla extract

½ cup (120 ml) whole milk, buttermilk*, or heavy cream, plus extra for brushing the tops

GLAZE
2 cups (250 g) confectioners' sugar

3 tablespoons whole milk or heavy cream

The flavor inspiration for these delectable dandies came from all over: Italy, my southern roots, my pantry staples, and my love of cheddar. Feel free to make up your own flavor combinations.

✦ Place the flour, sugar, and baking powder in a large bowl and whisk to combine.

✦ Grate the butter on the larger holes of a box (pastry) grater and add to the flour. If you don't have a box grater, add the butter to the flour mixture and, using two knives, cut the butter into the flour.

✦ Whisk the egg, vanilla, and milk together. Pour into the flour along with flavor option, if desired, and, using a fork, stir until just combined.

✦ Place the dough on a lightly floured surface and gently knead until the ingredients just start to come together. Pat into a 1½-inch-thick (4 cm thick) disk. Using a pastry cutter or chef's knife, cut the disk into 8 equal wedges. Place the wedges on a parchment-lined baking sheet and freeze for 15 minutes.

✦ While the scones chill, preheat the oven to 400°F (205°C). Brush the scones with the milk and bake for 18 to 20 minutes or until golden. Allow scones to cool for 15 minutes.

✦ In a medium bowl, whisk the confectioners' sugar and milk until smooth and creamy. Drizzle the glaze over the scones.

It's essential that the butter and dough remain cold while making the scones. This creates a super flaky and tender scone. Don't use a food processor, because it will create an over-processed, crumbly scone.

If you don't have buttermilk, add 1 tablespoon lemon juice or vinegar to 1 cup (240ml) minus 1 tablespoon milk, stir, and allow to sit for 5 minutes.

TO ENJOY LATER
Wrap then divide wedges of dough in parchment paper and refrigerate up to 3 days before baking. To freeze, place the wrapped pieces in zip-top bags for up to 3 months before baking.

PREP IN ADVANCE
The dry ingredients can be whisked and covered and stored. The wet ingredients can be combined and refrigerated overnight or until ready to bake.

FLAVOR OPTIONS

1. **Cacio e Pepe Scones:** Add ⅓ cup (30 g) grated Parmesan cheese and 1 teaspoon ground black pepper into the flour mixture. Before baking, sprinkle additional Parmesan on top of the scones plus a pinch of black pepper.

2. **Maple Bacon Scones:** Add ½ cup (115 g) cooked and finely chopped bacon into the flour mixture (reserve another 2 tablespoons/28 g) chopped bacon for the topping). For the glaze, mix together 2 cups (250 g) confectioners' sugar, 2 tablespoons milk or heavy cream, and 2 tablespoons maple syrup in a bowl. Glaze scones and sprinkle with additional bacon.

3. **Cheddar and Scallion, Chive, or Dill Scones:** Mix ½ cup (55 g) grated cheddar cheese and 2 tablespoons scallions, chives, or dill into the flour mixture. Sprinkle additional grated cheddar on top of the scones before baking.

4. **Dried Fruit and Nuts Scones:** Add ⅓ cup (45 g) chopped dried cranberries, cherries, or blueberries and ⅓ cup (40 g) chopped nut of choice into the flour mixture and continue according to directions. Glaze as directed.

PREP TIME
10 minutes

COOK TIME
1 hour

MAKES
1 loaf; 10 to 12 slices

Blender Banana Breakfast Loaf

Nonstick cooking spray

3 ripe bananas, mashed (about 1 cup/150 g)

1 cup (220 g) packed brown sugar

¾ cup (180 ml) olive oil

¼ cup (60 ml) sour cream

2 large eggs, at room temperature

1 tablespoon vanilla extract

3 cups (270 g) old-fashioned rolled oats (aka 5-minute oats)

2 teaspoons ground cinnamon

1 teaspoon baking soda

½ teaspoon kosher salt

1 cup (175 g) dark chocolate chips, plus a few extra for the top

1 tablespoon granulated sugar

So you thought a blender was only good for smoothies? This recipe can be thrown together in less than 10 minutes, plus, it's gluten-free.

✦ Preheat the oven to 350°F (175°C) and line a 9 by 5-inch (23 by 12 cm) loaf pan with parchment paper, crossing two strips to create an overhang on all 4 sides (so you have a sling to remove the loaf from the pan). Spray the parchment paper with nonstick cooking spray.

✦ Add the mashed bananas, brown sugar, olive oil, sour cream, eggs, vanilla, oats, 1 teaspoon cinnamon, baking soda, and salt into a high-speed blender. Process until the oats are fully broken down and the mixture is smooth.

✦ Remove the blender container from the machine, then carefully fold in the chocolate chips with a spatula. Pour the batter into the prepared pan, then sprinkle a few extra chocolate chips on top. Stir together the granulated sugar and cinnamon, and then sprinkle the mixture on top of the batter in an even layer.

✦ Bake in the preheated oven for 55 to 60 minutes, or until a toothpick inserted in the center comes out clean. Allow the bread to cool in the pan for 10 minutes. Use a knife to gently cut around the bread to make sure it doesn't stick to the sides of the pan. Turn the bread upside down onto your hand and place the bread bottom side down on a cooling rack.

If using frozen bananas, thaw them thoroughly before blending.

Craving banana bread, but you only have yellow bananas? Place them in a 350°F (175°C) oven on a rimmed sheet pan (poke a few holes in each one so they don't explode!) for about 15 minutes to bring out their natural sweetness. Allow the bananas to cool before starting this recipe.

There is no gluten in this bread, so it crumbles easily. Store it in the fridge after it's cooled so it's easier to slice.

TO ENJOY LATER

The baked bread can be cooled, wrapped in foil, and refrigerated for up to 3 days. To freeze, place the cooled loaf in a labeled zip-top bag for up to 4 months. When ready to eat, defrost them then microwave slices for 30 seconds, place in a preheated 250°F (120°C) oven for 5 minutes, or in a 350°F (175°C) air fryer for 2 minutes.

PREP IN ADVANCE

The dry ingredients can be whisked and stored covered. The wet ingredients can be stirred and refrigerated for up to 2 days.

PREP TIME
1 hour 15 minutes
(includes chilling the
dough)

COOK TIME
15 minutes

MAKES
20 large cookies

Colossal Peanut Butter Chocolate Cookies

2½ cups (315 g) all-purpose flour

1 teaspoon baking soda

1 teaspoon baking powder

½ teaspoon kosher salt

1 cup (2 sticks/450 g) unsalted butter, at room temperature

¾ cup (165 g) packed light or dark brown sugar

1 cup (200 g) granulated sugar

2 large eggs, at room temperature

¾ cup (180 ml) smooth or crunchy peanut or almond butter

1 teaspoon vanilla extract

1 cup (175 g) semi-sweet or dark (70%) chocolate disks, chunks, or chips

1 cup (210 g) chocolate candy pieces

½ cup (75 g) chopped peanuts or walnuts (optional)

I don't keep a lot of candy in the house, but chocolate candy pieces are what makes these pantry-friendly cookies so epic. I'm a big fan of the dye-free ones from Trader Joe's. Fruit and vegetable colors give them their vibrant hue.

✦ Place the flour, baking soda, baking powder, and salt in a medium bowl and whisk to thoroughly combine.

✦ Place the butter and sugars in a large bowl, if you're using a hand mixer, or in the bowl of a standing mixer, and beat for 3 to 4 minutes or until light in color, thick and creamy. Add the eggs, one at a time, and mix until incorporated, about one minute. Add the nut butter and vanilla and beat an additional minute or until combined. Slowly add the flour mixture, mixing until a dough forms. Add in ¾ cup (130 g) of the chocolate disks, ¾ cup (160 g) of the chocolate pieces, and the nuts, if using.

✦ Refrigerate the dough for 1 hour or cover and refrigerate overnight.

✦ Preheat the oven to 350°F (175°C). Line two or three large sheet pans with silicone liners or parchment paper. Use a large ice cream scoop to scoop 6 to 8 portions of cookie dough onto each sheet, making sure to space them out. Gently use your palm to press the center of each ball of dough down slightly and top with the remaining chocolate and candy pieces. Bake the cookies for 15 minutes or until slightly golden.

✦ Allow cookies to remain on the sheet pan for 5 minutes to settle before removing to a cooling rack.

While you can leave it for longer, I find that an hour is the perfect amount of time for the dough to chill in the refrigerator. There's a sweet spot, when the dough is soft, but not super firm, for scooping the dough onto sheet pans. If you leave it in the fridge too long and it feels too hard, just leave it out for 10 minutes before shaping the cookies.

TO ENJOY LATER

Store the cooled baked cookies in airtight containers or labeled zip-top bags for up to 4 days at room temperature or refrigerate for up to 7 days. To freeze, place the cooled cookies in glass jars or labeled zip-top bags in the freezer for up to 4 months.

PREP IN ADVANCE

The dough can be formed into balls, slightly flattened, frozen on a parchment-lined baking tray for 1 hour, and then placed in zip-top bags for up to 4 months. Bake as directed, adding 1 to 2 minutes to the total baking time.

Flourless Double-Chocolate Muffins

PREP TIME
10 minutes

COOK TIME
25 minutes

MAKES
12 muffins

1 cup (240 ml) applesauce

½ cup (120 ml) pure maple syrup

¼ cup (60 ml) full-fat coconut milk

¼ cup (60 ml) melted coconut oil

2 large eggs

1 teaspoon vanilla extract

2 cups (180 g) rolled oats

¼ cup (25 g) cocoa powder

1 teaspoon baking powder

½ teaspoon baking soda

½ teaspoon kosher salt

¾ cup (130 g) dark chocolate chips

This is a riff on another one of the all-time most popular recipes on Weelicious, my Flourless Pumpkin Chocolate Muffins. Instead of pumpkin, this version is made with applesauce, resulting in a light, moist, chocolate cake–like texture. I think they taste just like boxed chocolate cake mix, and I mean that in the BEST way possible.

✦ Preheat the oven to 350°F (175°C) and line a 12-cup (2.8 liter) muffin tin with muffin liners. In a high-speed blender, place the applesauce, maple syrup, coconut milk, coconut oil, eggs, vanilla, oats, cocoa powder, baking powder, baking soda, and salt. Process until the batter is smooth and the consistency of brownie batter.

✦ Add ½ cup (85 g) of the chocolate chips and stir into the batter by hand with a spatula, then pour the batter into the prepared muffin tin, filling each cavity up almost to the top. Top the muffins with the remaining ¼ cup (45 g) chocolate chips, adding a few to the top of each muffin.

✦ Bake for 20 to 25 minutes, or until a toothpick inserted in the center of a muffin comes out clean.

You can substitute baby food or pumpkin puree for the applesauce to achieve the same moist texture.

TO ENJOY LATER

After baking, store the cooled, tightly wrapped muffins at room temperature for up to 2 days or refrigerated for up to 3 days. To freeze, place the cooled muffins in labeled zip-top bags for up to 4 months. To rewarm, microwave for 30 seconds, or place in a preheated 250°F (120°C) oven for 5 minutes or in an air fryer at 350°F (175°C) for 2 minutes.

PREP IN ADVANCE

The dry ingredients can be whisked and left covered on a counter. The wet ingredients can be stirred, covered, and refrigerated overnight or until ready to bake.

PREP TIME
45 minutes (includes
chilling the dough)

COOK TIME
15 minutes plus time to
make the fillings

MAKES
16 single-serving pies

Sweet or Savory Hand Pies, Four Ways

½ cup (1 stick/55 g)
unsalted butter, at
room temperature

4 ounces (115 g) cream
cheese

¼ cup (60 ml) heavy
cream

1½ cups (190 g)
plus 3 tablespoons
all-purpose flour, plus
more for rolling out
dough

½ teaspoon kosher salt

Filling of choice (see
recipes on page 216)

1 large egg, whisked
with 1 tablespoon
water

2 tablespoons
granulated sugar or
sesame seeds

My friend Jules gets all the credit for this recipe, which is just the thing to make and freeze for those days when you need the perfect meal for one. It's equally great to make for a school picnic or potluck.

+ Place the butter, cream cheese, and heavy cream in a food processor and pulse to combine, about 1 minute. Add the flour and salt and pulse until a dough forms, about 30 seconds. Flatten the ball of dough into a thick disk, wrap in plastic wrap or parchment, and refrigerate for 30 to 60 minutes.

+ While the dough is chilling, preheat the oven to 400°F (205°C) and make your filling of choice.

+ Roll out the dough ⅛ to ¼ inch (3 to 6 mm) thick on a lightly floured work surface. Using a large 4-inch (10 cm) round cookie cutter or the rim of a drinking glass, cut out disks of dough. Combine and roll out the scraps of dough and cut out more disks until you have 16 in all.

+ Place 1 to 2 tablespoons of the filling on one-half of a dough round. Fold over the other half of the dough to create a half moon and use the tines of a fork to press down the edges of the dough to seal. Place the hand pies on a parchment- or silpat-lined baking sheet, allowing space in between, brush the tops with the egg wash, and sprinkle with sugar or sesame seeds. Bake the hand pies for 15 minutes or until golden.

You can use any seasonal fruits or vegetables to create your own fillings!

CONTINUES

TO ENJOY LATER

The baked pies can be cooled and then refrigerated in an airtight container for up to 3 days. To rewarm, place in a preheated 250°F (120°C) oven for 5 minutes or in an air fryer at 400°F (205°C) for 2 minutes.

PREP IN ADVANCE

The dough can be made up to 6 days ahead and stored in plastic wrap in the fridge. The filling can be made up to 3 days ahead and stored in the fridge in an airtight container. To freeze, place unbaked pies on a parchment-lined baking sheet and freeze for 1 hour. Transfer pies to labeled zip-top bags and freeze for up to 4 months. Bake as directed.

1. Spinach and Feta Filling

1 tablespoon olive oil

2 cloves garlic, chopped

12 ounces (340 g) fresh spinach, or 1 (10-ounce/280 ml) block frozen spinach, defrosted and thoroughly drained of excess water

½ teaspoon dried oregano

1 teaspoon kosher salt

½ cup (4 ounces/115 g) feta cheese

Heat the oil in a large sauté pan over medium heat, add the garlic, and sauté for 1 minute. Add the spinach, oregano, and salt and sauté for 2 minutes, until wilted. Drain off any excess liquid and cool. Stir in the feta.

2. Pizza Filling

1 cup homemade or jarred marinara or pizza sauce

1½ cups grated mozzarella cheese

1 cup diced pepperoni, olives, or cooked vegetables (optional)

Place all the ingredients in a bowl and stir to throughly combine.

3. Caramelized Onion and Mushroom Filling

2 tablespoons olive oil

1 small yellow onion, diced

1 cup mushrooms, sliced (white, cremini, shiitake, oyster, or any wild mushrooms work)

¼ teaspoon kosher salt

½ cup grated mozzarella cheese

Heat the oil in a large sauté pan over low to medium heat and cook the onions 15 minutes. Add the mushrooms and sauté for an additional 4 to 5 minutes or until the onions are caramelized and the mushrooms are soft and turning golden.

4. Berry Filling

1½ cups (about 12 ounces) berries (fresh or frozen blueberries, blackberries, raspberries, and/or hulled and chopped strawberries)

2 tablespoons sugar

1½ teaspoons cornstarch

1 teaspoon lemon zest

½ teaspoon vanilla extract

Place all the ingredients in a bowl and stir to thoroughly combine.

Panzanella, Four Ways

PREP TIME
15 to 20 minutes

COOK TIME
20 to 30 minutes

SERVES
4

CROUTONS

8 ounces (225 g) sourdough bread, cubed (about 5 cups)

1 tablespoon olive oil

Kosher salt and freshly ground black pepper

PANZANELLA DRESSING

Juice of 1 lemon

2 tablespoons red wine vinegar

½ shallot, minced

1 teaspoon honey

1 tablespoon Dijon mustard

Kosher salt and freshly ground black pepper

½ cup (120 ml) olive oil

Panzanella is an Italian salad usually comprised of bread, tomato, and onions, however I created four versions of it to demonstrate how versatile panzanella can be, especially when it comes to using what is in season or what you have access to. Start by making the croutons and the dressing, which are the same for each version, and then try switching up the salad ingredients. These are a few of my favorite combinations, but you can play around and find your own favorites!

✦ **Make the croutons:** Preheat the oven to 425°F (220°C). Spread out the bread cubes on a rimmed sheet pan. Drizzle with the olive oil, then season with salt and pepper. Toss gently with your hands to make sure the bread is evenly coated. Bake for 20 minutes, tossing halfway through to ensure even cooking, or until the bread is crisp and golden.

✦ **Make the dressing:** To a pint-size mason jar with a tight-fitting lid, add all of the dressing ingredients. Seal the jar and shake the contents until emulsified.

✦ Now it is time to make the salad. See below and following page for different flavor options!

Make a double batch of the dressing and keep half to use later as a dressing or marinade.

For perfect orange sections, use a sharp knife to remove the outer peel and pith. Cut between the sections, avoiding the membrane, removing just orange sections.

1. Peach and Corn Panzanella

1 tablespoon unsalted butter

2 cups (190 g) fresh or frozen corn kernels

Kosher salt

4 cups (80 g) loosely packed baby arugula

Freshly ground black pepper

3 peaches (or nectarines), pitted and thinly sliced

1 (8-ounce/ 225 g) ball fresh mozzarella, torn into bite-size pieces

✦ Melt the butter in a large skillet set over medium heat. Add the corn and a pinch of salt and cook until the corn begins to caramelize, stirring often, about 5 to 7 minutes. Set aside.

✦ Add the arugula, corn, and the prepared croutons to a large bowl. Add half of the prepared dressing and a pinch of salt and pepper and toss until the greens are well coated and the bread starts to absorb the dressing. Top with the peach slices and freshly torn mozzarella, then drizzle with the remaining dressing and serve.

CONTINUES

2. Radicchio and Winter Citrus Panzanella

3 Cara Cara or blood oranges*, rind and pith removed, sliced

2 cups (40 g) loosely packed baby arugula

1 head radicchio, cored and thinly sliced

1 fennel bulb, cored and thinly sliced

½ cup (65 g) pine nuts

Kosher salt and freshly ground black pepper

✦ Place the orange slices, arugula, radicchio, fennel, and pinenuts in a large bowl. Add half of the prepared dressing, tossing to coat. Add the prepared croutons, the remaining dressing, and a pinch of salt and pepper. Toss until the greens are well coated and the bread starts to absorb the dressing, then serve.

3. Kale and Squash Panzanella

1 medium acorn squash, halved, seeds discarded, cut into 1-inch (2.5 cm) pieces

1 tablespoon olive oil

Kosher salt and freshly ground black pepper

2 bunches lacinato kale, stems discarded, leaves thinly sliced

½ cup (70 g) sunflower seeds

½ cup (50 g) grated Parmesan cheese

✦ Preheat oven to 45°0F (230°C). Add the squash to a rimmed sheet pan and toss with the olive oil, then season with salt and pepper. Roast for 20 to 25 minutes, tossing the squash halfway through, until tender and golden. Set aside.

✦ Add the kale to a large mixing bowl. Add half of the prepared dressing to the kale, massaging it first with your hands to break down some of the fiber; it will become softer and reduce in volume. Add the roasted squash, sunflower seeds, grated Parmesan cheese, and the prepared croutons. Add the remaining dressing and a pinch of salt and pepper. Toss until well coated and the bread starts to absorb the dressing, then serve.

4. Asparagus and Pea Panzanella

Kosher salt

2 cups (290 g) fresh or frozen peas

1 bunch asparagus, woody ends trimmed and discarded, cut into 1-inch (2.5 cm) segments

4 cups (80 g) loosely packed baby spinach

Freshly ground black pepper

½ cup (50 g) grated Parmesan cheese

✦ Bring a medium pot of salted water to a boil and set up an ice bath. Add the peas and asparagus to the boiling water and cook for 2 minutes, or until bright green and crisp tender. Drain and place in the ice bath for 30 seconds to stop the cooking, then drain thoroughly and set aside.

✦ Add the baby spinach, blanched peas, asparagus, and the prepared croutons to a large bowl. Add half of the prepared dressing and a pinch of salt and pepper and toss until the greens are well coated and the bread starts to absorb the dressing. Top with the Parmesan cheese, drizzle with remaining dressing and toss again before serving.

Maple-Cinnamon Waffle French Toast

4 large eggs

½ cup (120 ml) whole milk or heavy cream

2 tablespoons maple syrup

½ teaspoon vanilla extract

1 teaspoon ground cinnamon

Pinch kosher salt

8 slices bread of choice (challah, sandwich, cinnamon raisin, Texas toast, and brioche are my go-tos)

Butter, for brushing the waffle iron

Toppings: fresh raspberries, blueberries, strawberries, or blackberries; whipped cream; maple syrup; chocolate chips

Nine out of ten days I've got milk, bread, and eggs in my kitchen, and lucky for me, this recipe, which combines two breakfast favorites, is one of my kids' most requested. Their idea of the perfect breakfast is two pieces of this waffle French toast, a handful of fresh strawberries, and maple syrup or fresh whipped cream on top. Just place the soaked bread inside the waffle iron to make the puffiest maple-soaked bread you've ever tasted and plenty of grooves to catch whatever you pour or place on top.

✦ Preheat the waffle iron.

✦ Whisk the eggs in a large shallow bowl. Whisk in the milk, maple syrup, vanilla, cinnamon, and salt to combine.

✦ Submerge the slices of bread, one at a time, into the egg mixture for 30 seconds, or until they absorb the mixture.

✦ Place a slice of the bread into the waffle iron and cook for 4 to 5 minutes, or until the bread turns golden and puffs. *(Alternatively, the French toast can be sautéed in a large skillet over medium heat for 2 minutes on each side or until golden.)*

✦ Top the French toast with maple syrup, fresh berries, whipped cream, or fried chicken if you're feeling extra jazzy.

As you finish cooking each waffle, you can place them on baking sheets and keep them warm in a preheated 250°F (120°C) oven until you are ready to serve them.

TO ENJOY LATER
The cooked French toast can be cooled and refrigerated in an airtight container for up to 3 days. To freeze, place cooled pieces of the toast in labeled zip-top bags in the freezer for up to 4 months. To rewarm, microwave for 30 seconds, or place in a preheated 250°F (120°C) oven for 5 minutes, or in an air fryer at 350°F (175°C) for 2 minutes, or in a toaster oven for 1 minute. Add an additional minute or so if warming frozen French toast.

PREP IN ADVANCE
Prepare the milk mixture the night before, storing it covered in the fridge, and then submerge the bread when ready to cook.

PREP TIME
15 minutes

COOK TIME
45 minutes

SERVES
4 to 6

Ribollita Soup

½ loaf favorite crusty bread, cut or torn into 1-inch (2.5 cm) pieces or cubes (about 2 cups)

6 tablespoons olive oil, plus extra for drizzling

1 small onion, diced

2 carrots, diced

3 celery stalks, diced

1½ teaspoons kosher salt

4 cloves garlic, minced

1 (28-ounce/795 g) can whole tomatoes with juice

1 (15-ounce/115 g) can white beans, drained and rinsed

4 cups (about 1 liter) vegetable stock

4 large leaves lacinato or Tuscan kale

1 small wedge Parmesan cheese with rind (about a 4-inch/ 10 cm piece), plus more grated for serving

1 fresh sprig of thyme or 1 teaspoon dried

Pinch crushed red pepper (optional)

Ribollita is a traditional Italian bread soup and a brilliant example of making use of what you have in your kitchen, including that magnificent Parmesan rind that you hopefully stowed away in your freezer for the day you would be making ribollita.

+ Preheat the oven to 350°F (175°C). Place the bread on a baking sheet and drizzle with 3 tablespoons of the olive oil. Bake for 15 to 20 minutes or until the bread starts to turn golden.

+ Heat the remaining 3 tablespoons olive oil in a large Dutch oven or pot over medium heat. Add the onion, carrots, celery, and salt and sauté for 7 minutes or until fork tender, stirring occasionally. Add the garlic and sauté for an additional minute. Add the tomatoes plus their juice, the beans, and stock.

+ Remove 1½ cups (360 ml) of the mixture to a blender or food processor to puree until smooth and then return the soup to the pot (or use an immersion blender to puree the soup on the stovetop).

+ Remove and discard the stems in the kale and tear the leaves into bite-size pieces. Add the Parmesan wedge, thyme, kale, and crushed red pepper, if using. Bring to a boil and reduce the heat to a simmer. Cover and cook for 15 to 20 minutes. *(Alternatively, if you've got a slow cooker, you can use it here. Cook the soup on high for 3 to 4 hours or on low for 6 to 8 hours. Use an immersion blender in the slow cooker or remove 1½ cups to a blender to puree and add back in.)*

+ Divide the soup among bowls, top with crunchy bread, a drizzle of olive oil, and more Parmesan, if desired.

Don't have celery? Fennel delivers a delightful flavor twist and will have everyone you're serving this soup to stumped as to what's in it. No bread, you say? You can substitute pasta, potatoes, or even double the beans and call it a classic minestrone.

If you don't have stock, feel free to substitute water.

TO ENJOY LATER

Before adding the bread, the soup can be cooled and refrigerated in an airtight container for up to 4 days, or divided between glass jars or freezer bags filled three-quarters full so they can expand when frozen for up to 4 months. Reheat the soup in the microwave or in a pot over low to medium heat until warmed through and then add the bread and any other toppings.

Crispy Avocado Tacos

PREP TIME
20 minutes

COOK TIME
10 minutes

SERVES
4 to 6

QUICK-PICKLED ONIONS

1 small red onion, thinly sliced

½ cup (120 ml) white vinegar

2 tablespoons sugar

2 teaspoons kosher salt

CILANTRO CREMA

½ cup (120 ml) Mexican crema or sour cream

¼ cup (7.5 g) loosely packed fresh cilantro (leaves and stems), finely chopped

Juice of 1 lime

⅛ teaspoon garlic powder

½ teaspoon kosher salt

TACOS

½ cup (80 g) rice flour or Wondra flour*

½ teaspoon ground cumin

½ teaspoon paprika

½ teaspoon garlic powder

1 teaspoon kosher salt

2 large ripe avocados, pitted, peeled, and sliced into 16 slices total

Olive, vegetable, avocado, or canola oil

4 to 6 corn tortillas

Toasted sesame seeds

I love avocados. Each week, my friend Jamila brings me ten perfect ones, a few of which I put aside to make these avocado tacos. Buttery inside and crispy outside, they are so satisfying. Just to get in a little extra protein and calcium, I add a shake of toasted sesame seeds, which gives them a slightly nutty flavor and texture to boot.

✦ **Make the pickled onions:** Place the onions in a large heatproof bowl or jar. In a small saucepan, bring the remaining pickle ingredients just to a boil, stirring to dissolve the sugar and salt. Allow to cool for 5 minutes, then pour the mixture over the onions. Let cool completely and refrigerate for up to 2 months.

✦ **Make the crema:** In a small bowl, mix together all the crema ingredients until well combined.

✦ **Make the tacos:** In a medium bowl, whisk the rice flour, cumin, paprika, garlic powder, and salt. Place avocado slices one at a time in the flour mixture, covering both sides and tapping off the excess. Remove to a plate. Add ½ cup (120 ml) water to the remaining flour mixture to create a wet batter and dip the avocado slices in one at a time.

✦ Heat a large sauté pan over medium-high heat and add a thin layer of oil. Add the avocado slices and cook for 3 to 4 minutes on each side or until golden on both sides.

✦ To assemble the tacos, place a tortilla on a plate, top with two or three slices of fried avocado, some cilantro crema, pickled onions, and toasted sesame seeds. Repeat with the remaining ingredients.

If you've got whitefish fillets in the fridge or freezer, make fish tacos! Pat them dry to remove any extra moisture, slice into pieces, and prepare in the same way as the avocado.

Don't have Wondra or rice flour? Whisk together ½ cup all-purpose flour and ½ teaspoon cornstarch.

TO ENJOY LATER
Pickled onions are great on sandwiches, salads, or any dish that needs more zip and zing.

PREP IN ADVANCE
The cilantro crema can be prepared up to 3 days in advance and stored in a covered container in the fridge. The flour mixture can be prepared up to 3 days ahead and set aside at room temperature.

Quesadillas, Four Ways

4 large flour tortillas

3 cups (330 g) grated mozzarella cheese (about ¾ cup/85 g per quesadilla)

Quesadillas are their own food group in our house. While simple mozzarella cheese is our general go-to filling, if I really, really want to jazz them up, I lean toward these variations. Thicker than your average quesadilla, sandwiching a host of surprising ingredients, they can be served at breakfast, lunch, or dinner and pretty much guarantee smiling faces all around.

Heat a large sauté pan (preferably cast iron) over medium-high heat. Place a tortilla in the skillet and scatter a handful of cheese on one side of the tortilla. Top with the optional ingredients and more cheese. Fold the other half of the tortilla over the fillings and gently press down to adhere. Cook the quesadilla for 2 to 3 minutes and toast until golden. Flip over to cook the other side for 2 to 3 minutes or until tortilla is golden and cheese is melted. Remove the quesadilla to a cooling rack where it will stay crisp while remaining quesadillas are cooked. Slice each quesadilla into 3 to 4 triangles and serve with desired toppings.

Quesadillas turn into magic when served with guacamole, salsa, pico de gallo, marinara, pesto, or even hot sauce.

FLAVOR OPTIONS

1. **Spicy Avocado Quesadillas:** Add 2 avocados, pitted and sliced, and drizzled with Sriracha or favorite hot sauce, on top of the grated cheese.

2. **Wild Mushroom, Spinach, and Triple-Cheese Quesadillas:** Add ½ cup (145 g) cooked shiitake or baby portobello mushrooms, 1 cup (225 g) cooked spinach, and use any mix of cheeses you enjoy (such as mozzarella, Monterey Jack, cheddar, etc.) as the filling.

3. **Bacon and Egg Quesadillas:** Place 4 pieces cooked and crumbled bacon and 4 scrambled eggs, divided between the 4 tortillas, on top of the grated cheese.

4. **Tomato Sauce and Pepperoni Quesadillas:** Spoon ½ cup (120 ml) marinara or pizza sauce and add 12 slices pepperoni divided between the 4 tortillas.

TO ENJOY LATER

Cooked quesadillas can be cooled and refrigerated in an airtight container up to 3 days. To freeze, place the cooked, cooled quesadillas in labeled zip-top bags for up to 4 months. To rewarm, microwave for 30 seconds, or place in a preheated 250°F (120°C) oven for 5 minutes, or in a 350°F (175°C) air fryer for 2 minutes, or in a saucepan over medium heat for 2 minutes.

A Month of Meal Prep

This is a guide for how to plan out an entire month of easy, delicious meals utilizing recipes in this book. Sunday is a prep day, the time for you to set yourself up for a week of success. As everyone likes to cut loose once a week, you'll notice that I left out Saturday. That's your time

WEEK ONE

SUNDAY

Summer Vegetables with Lemon Yogurt-Gremolata Dip (page 119)
* **MAKE & REFRIGERATE**

Green Goddess Dressing (page 131)
* **MAKE & REFRIGERATE (FOR WEEKS 1–3)**

Pasta
* **COOK 1½ LBS, TOSS WITH OLIVE OIL & REFRIGERATE**

Chocolate Granola Breakfast Cookies (page 204)
* **MAKE & STORE ½ IN AIRTIGHT CONTAINER, FREEZE ½ (FOR WEEK 3)**

Ribollita Soup (page 223)
* **MAKE & REFRIGERATE ½, FREEZE ½ (FOR WEEK 4)**

Freezer-Stash Breakfast Burritos (page 66)
* **MAKE & FREEZE (FOR WEEK 2)**

Croutons (page 217)
* **MAKE A DOUBLE BATCH**

Any Green Pesto (page 132)
* **MAKE & STORE ½ IN FRIDGE, FREEZE ½ (FOR WEEK 4)**

Creamy Chia Pudding (page 71)
* **MAKE & REFRIGERATE**

Colossal Peanut Butter Chocolate Cookies (page 210)
* **MAKE & STORE ½ IN AIRTIGHT CONTAINER, FREEZE ½ (FOR WEEK 3)**

MONDAY

Maple-Cinnamon Waffle French Toast (page 220) *freeze ½ (for Week 3)	**Breakfast**
Green salad with ½ Summer Vegetables + Green Goddess Dressing	**Lunch**
Dijon, Honey, and Garlic Hasselback Chicken Breast (page 83) + Smashed Potatoes with Crispy Capers (page 124)	**Dinner**

TUESDAY

Chocolate Granola Breakfast Cookies	**Breakfast**
Ribollita Soup *reheat refrigerated ½	**Lunch**
Zippy Fish Tacos (page 151)	**Dinner**

WEDNESDAY

Double-Chocolate Protein Smoothie (page 72) *freeze leftovers into popsicles	**Breakfast**
Freezer-Stash Breakfast Burritos *reheat from fridge	**Lunch**
Panzanella (page 217) *pick 1 of 4 ways + use ½ croutons	**Dinner**

THURSDAY

Chia Pudding	**Breakfast**
Pasta with ½ Summer Vegetables + Any Green Pesto *use cooked pasta	**Lunch**
Turkey and Quinoa Chili (page 103) with green salad + Green Goddess Dressing *make double + freeze ½ (for Week 3)	**Dinner**

FRIDAY

Chocolate Raspberry Sheet-Pan Pancake (page 68) *freeze ½, cut into squares (for Week 4)	**Breakfast**
½ Croutons with dip (hummus, PB and J, etc.) + your favorite frozen vegetables, defrosted, with Green Goddess Dressing	**Lunch**
Kitchen Sink Pasta (page 176) *use cooked pasta	**Dinner**

to relax, go out to eat, take a day off from cooking or make something spontaneous. Finally, I recommend making dessert on Sunday to serve during the week as you see fit. After all, you know better than me when you need it!

WEEK TWO

SUNDAY

Easy Overnight Belgian Waffles (page 76)
✳ **PREP BATTER FOR MONDAY**

Mushroom, Spinach, and Pinto Bean Enchiladas (page 164)
✳ **MAKE & REFRIGERATE**

Apple Cinnamon Steel-Cut Oatmeal (page 199)
✳ **MAKE & REFRIGERATE
(CAN ALSO MAKE MORNING OF)**

Creamy Balsamic Vinaigrette (page 128)
✳ **MAKE & REFRIGERATE**

Classic Chicken Soup (page 89)
✳ **MAKE & REFRIGERATE**

Sauté 6 Cups Your Favorite Vegetables
✳ **MAKE & REFRIGERATE**

Black Bean Brownie Cookies (page 175)
✳ **STORE ½ IN AIRTIGHT CONTAINER & FREEZE ½
(FOR ANOTHER WEEK)**

MONDAY

Overnight Belgian Waffles *freeze ½ (for Week 4)	Breakfast
Sheet-Pan Tofu (pages 108–115) *pick 1 of 4 ways	Lunch
Mushroom, Spinach, and Pinto Bean Enchiladas *reheat	Dinner

TUESDAY

Apple Cinnamon Steel-Cut Oatmeal *reheat (or make)	Breakfast
Green salad using anything in fridge with Creamy Balsamic Vinaigrette	Lunch
Classic Chicken Soup with crusty bread or crackers	Dinner

WEDNESDAY

Freezer-Stash Breakfast Burritos *reheat from freezer	Breakfast
½ Sautéed Vegetables with Green Goddess Dressing	Lunch
Cauliflower Fried Rice (page 136)	Dinner

THURSDAY

Any Veggie Frittata (page 60) *using ½ Sautéed Vegetables	Breakfast
Quesadillas (page 227) *pick 1 of 4 ways	Lunch
Grilled Pork Tenderloin with Chimichurri (page 99) + Smashed Brussels Sprouts (page 123) *double sprouts recipe + refrigerate ½ for tomorrow	Dinner

FRIDAY

Ricotta Soft-Scrambled Eggs (page 63)	Breakfast
Air-Fried Coconut Shrimp (page 156) with Smashed Brussels Sprouts	Lunch
The BEST Chicken Burger (page 84) with salad + Creamy Balsamic Vinaigrette	Dinner

WEEK THREE

SUNDAY

Blueberry-Cornmeal Breakfast Cake (page 148)
  ✳ **PREP & REFRIGERATE**

Savory Hand Pies (page 214)
  ✳ **BAKE, FREEZE ½ (FOR WEEK 4)
  & REFRIGERATE ½**

Brown Rice
  ✳ **MAKE 5 COOKED CUPS**

Blender Banana Breakfast Loaf (page 209)
  ✳ **BAKE & STORE IN AIRTIGHT CONTAINER**

Cauliflower with Olive-Caper Vinaigrette
(page 120)
  ✳ **MAKE & REFRIGERATE**

Lemon-Herb Compound Butter (page 135)
  ✳ **MAKE & REFRIGERATE**

Leftover Rice Pudding (page 187)
  ✳ **MAKE USING RICE ABOVE (OR CAN BE
  MADE ANY NIGHT OF WEEK)**

MONDAY

Blueberry-Cornmeal Breakfast Cake	Breakfast
Savory Hand Pies + salad with Creamy Balsamic Vinaigrette	Lunch
Lime Pulled Chicken (page 79) + avocado slices + steamed brown rice	Dinner

TUESDAY

Blender Banana Breakfast Loaf	Breakfast
Cheesy Brown Rice Cakes (page 184) *make using leftover cooked rice	Lunch
Salmon with Lemon-Herb Butter (page 155) + Cauliflower with Olive-Caper Vinaigrette + salad with Green Goddess Dressing	Dinner

WEDNESDAY

Toasted bagel or favorite bread with Compound Butter	Breakfast
Lime Pulled Chicken over brown rice + Cauliflower with Olive-Caper Vinaigrette	Lunch
Crispy Avocado Tacos (page 224)	Dinner

THURSDAY

Chocolate Granola Breakfast Cookies *remove from freezer night before; warm	Breakfast
Wild Mushroom Bean Bowl (page 160)	Lunch
Crispy Salmon Burgers (page 159) + sliced seasonal fruit	Dinner

FRIDAY

Chocolate Raspberry Sheet-Pan Pancake *reheat from frozen	Breakfast
Turkey & Quinoa Chili *reheat from frozen	Lunch
Crispy Chicken Thighs with Artichokes, Lemon, and Herbs (page 90)	Dinner

WEEK FOUR

SUNDAY

Mango Morning Glory Muffins (page 143)
* ✳ **BAKE, FREEZE ½ (FOR NEXT MONTH) & STORE ½ IN AIRTIGHT CONTAINER**

Summer Vegetables
* ✳ **MAKE & REFRIGERATE**

Brown Rice
* ✳ **MAKE 5 COOKED CUPS**

Stuffed Peppers (page 192)
* ✳ **MAKE STUFFING & REFRIGERATE**

Peanut Butter and Chocolate Olive Oil Granola (page 203)
* ✳ **BAKE & STORE IN AIRTIGHT CONTAINER**

Scones (page 206)
* ✳ **MAKE 1 VERSION, FREEZE ½ (FOR NEXT MONTH) & STORE ½ IN AIRTIGHT CONTAINER**

Any Fruit Crisp (page 147)
* ✳ **PREP & REFRIGERATE UP TO 2 DAYS**

MONDAY

Mango Morning Glory Muffins	Breakfast
½ Summer Vegetables with Lemon Yogurt–Gremolata Dip (page 119)	Lunch
Stuffed Peppers	Dinner

TUESDAY

Peanut Butter Chocolate Olive Oil Granola + greek yogurt + handful of strawberries	Breakfast
Savory Hand Pies *defrost & heat	Lunch
Shrimp and Artichoke Fra Diavolo (page 152)	Dinner

WEDNESDAY

Pull-Apart Egg Sandwiches with Crispy Prosciutto & Pesto (page 64) *use pesto from Week 1	Breakfast
Summer Vegetables with Lemon Yogurt–Gremolata Dip over brown rice + salad greens	Lunch
Blistered Cherry Tomato and Gooey Mozzarella Spaghetti (page 179) *refrigerate ½	Dinner

THURSDAY

Scones	Breakfast
Ribollita Soup *reheat from frozen	Lunch
Go-To Bibimbap (page 188) *use cooked brown rice	Dinner

FRIDAY

Easy Overnight Belgian Waffles *reheat from frozen	Breakfast
Crispy Artichoke Hearts with Caesar Dip (page 139) + Blistered Cherry Tomato & Gooey Mozzarella Spaghetti *reheat leftover spaghetti	Lunch
Sheet-Pan Sausage and Peppers (page 95) *double recipe, refrigerate & use for a lunch next week	Dinner

Recipe List

Refrigerator

Air Fry Every Day

Easily (and heathfully) add crispy deliciousness to your meals by cooking in an air fryer! The recipes below are ideal for air frying, but I always provide alternative cooking methods if you don't have one.

Acknowledgments

The Weelicious community: I am blessed to be a part of the most supportive virtual community any creator could hope to have. When I started this journey, I had no idea where it would lead, but looking back, I see that it was led by all of you. Your encouragement, questions, and willingness to share inspired me on this path that has always felt much more like a calling than a career. I feel like we've gone through parenthood together. Thank you for letting me into your lives.

Alison: The most incredible agent (and mother hen) a girl could ask for. I'm so grateful I get to walk hand in hand with you every step of the way.

Laura D: The editor so nice I've worked with her twice—and how lucky I am. Thank you for allowing me to create the book that I needed in my life and for your brilliant insight, guidance, and ability to help me through even the most difficult parts of the process with such a sense of calm.

Colin: Speaking of twice, photographing these last two books with you has been my favorite part of the process both times. Whatever I may have in my head never compares to what it looks like seen through your eyes. You treat every image like it's the most important one, and I have learned so much watching you work. Your talent knows no bounds.

Laura P: If you were a sushi chef, I would eat at your restaurant every night—and only order the omakase. From the moment I realized you were behind virtually all of my favorite book designs, I think I willed you into my life. Seeing your magic sprinkled throughout these pages fills me with pure joy. I'm forever your fangirl.

Deb, Mamie, Danielle, Natasha, Asha: The Abrams dream team! Handing your book over can feel like entrusting someone with your child, and you always make me feel like mine is in the best of hands. Thank you for putting so much time, effort, creativity—as well as your hearts—into this book and treating it like it was your own.

Marian: You (and Possum). Heaven. Everything you touch turns to gold and every image in this book proves it. Whenever I think about those two perfect weeks we spent together shooting this book, it immediately brings a smile to my face. You and your brilliant team—including Veronica, Jessica, and Natalie—are rock stars.

Amander: Not just another pretty face. You're a true jack-of-all-trades and lean fully into everything you do you with a smile.

Rachel: My wingwoman! My work wife! My ace in the hole! Dreaming, planning, and building with you fills my bucket and feeds my soul. You're a true superhero.

Hayley: The first time I met you I knew you were the one. I was right.

Molly: Thank you for your bright ideas, openness, collaboration, experimentation, sincerity, and warmth. I'd work with you over and over again.

Cheryl: A rite of passage some thirteen-year-old girls is a bat mitzvah. For me, it was meeting you.

Amy: Gurl, you have sick taste.

Clea & Joanna: You blessed my home with your brilliance when you first started, and helped show me that within organization lies magic.

I'd like to thank my good friends Robert and Nick at **Melissa's Produce** and Melissa at **Wean Green**, as well as **Spice It Your Way** (Zee), **Organic Valley** (Brian), **Eden Foods** (Robin), **Brightland** (Nora & Grace), **Simply Organic** (Taylor), **Prepdeck** (Alyssa), **Austin Baby Collection** (Kelly), and the team at **Vital Farms** for their generous support in the creation of this book.

My girlfriends (you know who you are): My village is small but mighty. I lean on you for so much and not only are you are always there, you inspire me at every turn.

(Mom + Dad)^2: My grandparents were everything to me as a child and I could not be more fortunate as my kids have the four best on the planet. Thank you for being so giving and for always being there with your love, faith, and boundless wisdom.

Kenya, Chloe, and Gemma: My *raison d'être.* You inspire me to be the best I can be.

Jon: There's no greater partner in the world. The yin to my yang. I wouldn't have it any other way. And if you ever leave me, I'll come find you. I love you.

Index

Editor: Laura Dozier
Design Manager: Danielle Youngsmith
Managing Editor: Glenn Ramirez
Production Manager: Sarah Masterson Hally

Book design by Laura Palese

Library of Congress Control Number:
2022946055

ISBN: 978-1-4197-6432-5
eISBN: 978-1-64700-618-1

Text copyright © 2023 Catherine McCord
Photographs copyright © 2023 Colin Price

Cover © 2023 Abrams

Published in 2023 by Abrams, an imprint of
ABRAMS. All rights reserved. No portion of
this book may be reproduced, stored in a
retrieval system, or transmitted in any form
or by any means, mechanical, electronic,
photocopying, recording, or otherwise,
without written permission from the publisher.

Printed and bound in the United States

10 9 8 7 6 5 4 3 2 1

Abrams books are available at special
discounts when purchased in quantity
for premiums and promotions as well as
fundraising or educational use. Special
editions can also be created to specification.
For details, contact specialsales@
abramsbooks.com or the address below.

Abrams® is a registered trademark of
Harry N. Abrams, Inc.

ABRAMS The Art of Books
195 Broadway, New York, NY 10007
abramsbooks.com